I0748449

TACHYON

TACHYON

TACHYON

William F. DeVault

ISBN: 1-7349469-2-5
ISBN-13: 978-1-7349469-2-5

To my children, both literarily and biologically.

Contents

A very brief introduction

While I was assembling this volume my brother, Robert, passed. It was quick and on his own terms. But, as always, we mourned not his passing but our loss. So I wrote the poem that starts this collection, bound to speak the arrogant truth that we don't know everything in this life and that platitudes and attitudes that bring us comfort are not always anything more than schoolyard fables.

I write this in the middle of the Coronavirus pandemic, fortunate not to have succumbed, but eventually mortality will work its way with this waystation, this pupa to the nature of the human soul. It gives me comfort against the terror of the oblivion that is an easy illusion for the end of life. I may outlive another generation or pass midsentence as I write this.

In any case, read on and live. Feel. Dream. Believe. And for some of you, when you look inside you will find not only me, but you yourself looking back at you, faster than light and faster than life.

Believe.

William F. DeVault

December 2020

for my brother, as he accelerates

there are no more mysteries for you
the sky is white and the night is a dimly remembered joke.

truth is, at last, obvious, and pain is an abstract concept.
afterlife is the all that was held back by the shadows.

the memories are there, but less relevant that expected,
as you find the frame is not as Sunday school prestidigitation.
but words that dissolve like sugar cubes in an April rain
plainly sweet but pure and sure of the vision expanded.

I envy you, the awareness and the peace of release
beyond any numbing drink or the stink of sorrows
borrowed to make you feel less than you were
but more than you imagined as you emerge, wings formed.

the caterpillars mourn their brethren, heathens of the ascension
as the pretention stands as hobbling prevention of freedoms
we are heir to, and they wonder why I smiled at your funeral.
the mind without the biochemical bounds that inhibit us.

there are no more mysteries for you
the sky is white and the night is a dimly remembered joke.

truth is, at last, obvious, and pain is an abstract concept.
afterlife is the all that was held back by the shadows.

Trick of the Night

a trick of the light, the night becomes you
and the shadows take on a pure and prurient hue.
how you twist and turn, burning my yearning as I am held
in rapt rapture, captured by your grace and the darkness
as it bids my imagination to focus on your form
without detail but with a sense of the center
of my desires, fires licking like greedy tongues
across your silhouette, wet with anticipation.
Hungry, even if held at bay, for now.

evidence

you dance in perfect meditation, releasing your unceasing joy
and those flickers of shyness, of hesitation, forgetting
that there are those who would judge you in selfish envy,
expressing their cruel spite in disregard when your every move
proves more eloquently than any theologian that there is a God.

The Sacraments

Baptism

Let the waters pool in the river in preparation for the ritual purification.
Transcending the acts of transgressive pasts, lasting long enough
to wash away all sorrows if you let it penetrate the waxy scale
we shield ourselves with, the lies of self-preservation, for we are not
alone in this world. Bare skin purged of sweat of fear and folly,
prepared for the entry of an Holy Spirit, incarnated as a lover,
who hovers over the water, drawing up the resinous ruins
and purifying it in a reign and rain of redemption, the purification
of what we were that we may live again, twice born.

Confession

Forgive me, for I have sinned.
I have lain with false idols, not knowing you were out there,
calling my name in subtle somnolences. The pretense bared
only when you spoke my name, that once, naked and open,
calling me down from the heavens to lay with you, flames
licking and burning away all doubts in a moment, no apologies
for the fiery furnace unleashed to consume the past, the present,
and to leave a field of cleansed ashes for a future altar.
I confess my transgressions and ask your forgiveness,
bless me with your kisses and touch, prepare me for Heaven.
I would be made worthy of your divine presence in my soul.

Communion and Absolution

I will take the flesh and the wine, divine, into me and make it a part of me.
Transubstantiating your essence in heated flesh and the blood of your desire
into a purifying agent to make me yours, to prove and purpose my redemption.

Your blood, mingled with sweat and the essence of your fragrant regions,
a taste like jasmine and the iron of my conviction to your divinity. I accept
the absolution of your surrender to my thirst and hunger. My passion.

And I, to you. Take my flesh into you and draw out the warm wine,
the leper's blood of my surrender to your tender and urgent needs, seed
given as feast, released, and we have taken two separate souls and merged.

Drink deeply, consume completely, leave nothing of this vessel,
for it is nothing without you to draw it in, sharing again your flesh and blood
as you swallow me, hollow me, and refill me with your transcendent spark.

Confirmation

my words you heard at the peak of my ecstasy hold true in the shallow shadows
of a room where there is no artificial heat or need to play pretense.
I would love you even had I not just melted into you, leaving part of me forever,
and I will still worship at this altar if the veil falls and I am cast out and away.
this was not a little boy playing at manhood. this was a lover, unlike any other
you have probably encountered. ministering his faith into you, and drawing hope
that you will confirm that this was more than another sawdust trail conversion.
do you reject the madness of this graceless age, where our Gods are all artificial?
will the laying on of our hands and lips kiss away all issues and doubts,
the stigma and stigmata of our self-imposed exile from the mediocrity?
speak me words of your heart, true, mine are constant and are of love for you.

Matrimony

the apple harvest.
the earnest offer made.
your answer holds my soul.

Last Rites

I am sworn unto death to love you. And beyond if permitted.
I will not love you as long as you live, but as I do, assured.
So here we are at last. Mortals. Lovers. Friends. The vows avowed said
to trust without doubt or fail, love for as long as time is measured.
I would feel your hands on my face one last time, breath on my skin, warm.
It matters not who passes first, but that we find ourselves again
within arm's reach of one another, I will miss your gentle form,
curled into me and sleeping like an ardent angel, far from sin
and far from those who would pluck her wings in envy and I will dance
alone with my memories of you. Frail essence of dreams, next to
the truth that I had not loved like this before we kissed at distance.
You are as beautiful as Summer, as perfect as Spring, and you
will always be my inamorata, no matter the day or season.
I found love to measure God against. Peace and joy in your passion.

Ordination

Ecce ego vobiscum sum omnibus diebus, usque ad consummationem sæculi.
An evangelist from a ronin, made by your love and his faith in it.
Dreams subject to the wind, but strong enough to tack and track the future.

I accept the commission, whether it be to your bedchambers or the night.
The cold stones are small comfort compared to your tender kisses, my love,
but I am given to this ordination, this extraordinary moment of grace.

I will feel the cold winds and the sharp stones that will be my bed while I await
your signal at the window that I may re-enter the city and claim my place,
beside you, before you, the more you dare, the more I care.

We will conquer all that before was too much for one alone to overcome.
We will conquer all that before was too much for one alone to understand.
We will conquer all that before was too much, but never again, my love.

This is a defining time, a shibboleth for the true romantics, awakening
slowly. One by one they come, then two by two as they are reacquainted
and the night fills with dancers and lovers and the voices of poets.

The sacraments have been taken, the vows made unbreakable if we will them
to be more than just words. Poets. Amomancers. Dreamers and weavers
of life and of the purity and surety of the passion you have returned to the world.

Ecce ego vobiscum sum omnibus diebus, usque ad consummationem sæculi.
This is our world, our world to explore and lay together and speak of what we have found,
sounding out the worlds of corners of life where no old worlds existed.

I am your priest, your preacher, your acolyte, your pope raised from an heretic
who had lost his way and will and had forgotten love, as he had been forgotten.
And then you came to me and made gentle words into amomancies to heal me.

I am stronger now. Still feeling and reeling from the scars of the unrepentant
who do not understand the nature of this brandywine, this heady intoxication
drawn in sweat and sweeter rain from the tempest of your body, into me.

We are lovers. And we shall reach for the heavens with renewed hope and faith.
We are lovers. And we shall teach all that heaven flows with renewed faith and hope.
We are lovers. And we shall teach all that heaven is now resident on this earth.

Kiss me and be slow and meticulous in your touch, awaken me at any hour
to call me to you, to demand I execute the sacraments again to prove my love.
I will not turn away from this joyous duty, I am purposed to your happiness.

I have been shaped to fit the curve of your body, the bend of your soul
and the darkness within you is of relevance to me, for I do not leave poison
in the wounds that they may not heal sufficiently, I will take it into me.

Ecce ego vobiscum sum omnibus diebus, usque ad consummationem sæculi.
I am a patient evangelist in your name. Bless me and empower me again.
And again. And again. I will share my sacraments and thank God for your existence.

Passages of Time in Words said to Me

I. Psyche

"I don't want to see the man I love
grow old and bitter
because poetry is never coming back."

Your words. Not mine.
My words were carefully chosen
in a threnody against past affections.

I have my moments, of course,
where I wish a well-crafted and resonant villanelle
could sell well enough to buy a house.

A house like the one I gave to my first wife
when I bet my heart and art on a passing fancy
(not mine, but another's) and found my way to the angels.

II. Brigit

"Come here," you said, in a red-headed growl of desire.
I wasn't about to argue, consumed by my own ardor -
even awe of this goddess of consummate fire
stretched out before me like a new frontier to explore.

III. a host of ghosts

…so many times the confession door was locked from the inside
and I was not given vital information before the rodeo.
by then, too late, as patterns of imprinting burned
with hormonocentric permanence bound me
with damn near immutability
with a stage-two illusion of romance.

IIII. Leopard

"You'd take a bullet for anyone."
That ended the argument as a simplistic statement on my ethos
tried to guilt-filter the very essence of who and what I am,
for better or worse, had made you strip naked and come on to me on the road
just outside of Tucson, with you wired on scoops of pharmaceuticals,
and you convinced me, eventually, that I was more than a deus ex machina
for fleeing home and your city of burned bridges and disappointments.

V. White Sunday

"I meant it when I said it."
of course the irony of you saying it
was not lost on me, the cost to me
was felt deeply in the velvet folds of my heart
where I had set aside pride and possibilities
to, not pursue, but follow an orphaned offer
because I did not understand that to some people
words lack permanence, like cheeseburger kisses
and fellatio for a lobster. and three black diamonds.

and the violence of indifference.

VI. Psyche II

"but I might die tonight."
I know you were just quoting Cat Stevens,
but the message was intimate and urgent.
beautiful validation for the petals to reach out
and draw the nourishment from the sun and air.
I admit, when the sky is still and I am contemplative
I recall not just your words, but your expression
and the sweet, urgent, tenderness of the day
when I had no defenses. and didn't want them.

VII. Heresy

"you don't need to be in love to love."
I believed, I was relieved, yet I grieved the fading lights
against the venomous sun, burning a thatch work patch work
to shield us from the falling stars we threw into the sky to die.
that there should be Diogenes' sister, in denim skirt and flowers
flowers flowers everywhere, not just your renegade air.
the petty, sweaty illusions that pull groin and gravity
to draw us inexplicably together.
I do believe in love at first sight, even if I fight against it,
a trapped, sapped animal, with just enough strength to pull free,
even if leaving a metaphorical leg or segment of memory.
I am a romantique. waiting in a garden that is scented
with the flowers and seven powers that have torn and reborn
a grave slave to the bloodlust and tender thrust awakening dust
in a crypt that has never held anything but the dreams of the damned
and the passions that only intensify in the abattoir of every lie I've ever been told.
I am the priest and the heretic. the lover and the hermit. the minstrel and martyr.

resurrect

laying down a beating where I'd been eating crow.
the blows are soft flesh on shattered sapphire.
too many business cards from timid MFAs,
mediocrities polluting Apollonian streams of consciousness.
I am sorry that your husband died.
I acknowledge that you loved him,
and he, you, and I am grateful you found joy
to your own side of the Pillars of Heracles.
the fates did not hate us
but allowed us to stumble in blind bindings
until we crumbled under the weight of our best pretensions.
cornbread corners to the hollow plates of desire.
I was unaware of the demon I found and bound
only with your persistent assistance. born of dragons
and chained in cinnabar and pitchblende. pitchfork tongue
and the dung of desecration, left in the garden.
he calls for you from within his cell, where I starve him
with distractions and abstractions while awaiting the resurrection
in a reinvented
winter that comes for us all
calling us liars as the fires fade
and we are paid up beyond the end of the stay
we had envisioned when we bought the condoms.
the halls and walls are as I envisioned them
described in the romantique's whispers
using words unheard in the most ancient places
where the Greek girl said I would find redemption.
she was wrong, but drunk at the time,
and I do not lay with the mysteries of Dionysius.
fire fire fire inspire desire conspire with the smaller mind
blinded by a scent of honeysuckle and night blooming jasmine.
reeling at the feeling of a greater death, of self, beyond logic
and the toxic remembrances that are mangled and tangled.
I gave up science and the truth of numbers
when I found that I would be always bound
by lesser minds, finding no freedom to discover
to uncover the essence of this transient life.

If God wants me dead

If God wants me dead
He knows where to find me so as
to bind me to an impossible task, to ask of me more than the all
that He ordained and I built upon as foundation

I confess I am not, physically, immortal, too many moving parts
creak and seek a gentle rest often enough that I can tell
there is great discussion between my cells and bells
as to when would be a good time to rebel against my will
and toss me in a gutter with a flutter and a sputter

I've no illusion of winning the argument against entropy
but a stalling action is another thing, altogether.

obscure

you have no idea my passions towards you, dark and liquid,
flowing in a knowing dream that I entertain even when you face me
certain that the curtains behind my eyes obscure the pantomime
of your body and heart, shared in a shocking revelation as I smile and nod
and the rush of blood tells me you have enchanted me into dreams
that I long thought bound and buried in preconscious meanders
salamanders of a ruby plasma flickering in nightmares nickering
to the notion of emotions manifest in untested theories of endurance.

I am darker than you imagine, hungry as only a monk who has fasted
for more than forty days and forty nights can appreciate, remembering
the texture and taste of jasmine and honey, the heat and the attar
of surrendered common-sense cast into the fires of desire for a rite
of repeated resurrection to your acceptance and transcendence.
diamond dispensations and the sensations of the ascendant captured
in gossamer nets of word and kiss and the friction of Egyptian cotton.

obscure to all but Polyphemus

I mean you no harm, but to charm you with treasonable fantasies
unlocked and cocked like a shotgun satyr, ridden when bidden
by thoughts neither one of us at one time considered reasonable,
our diptych flesh meshing in a search for a perch exquisite, hidden
only to those beyond these walls, for in this forthright night
we shall whisper passions requiring the inspiring light of heat
met with epic thirst and cursed to Polyphemus' sight
knowing our fates but in the moment not caring beyond the sweet
the salty the smooth the curved the brisance of resonance
when diaphanous barriers fall away to lie no more as surrogates
and we smother our consciences in preconscious natures' dance
as we seek to build pyres of scented skin and hungers consummate.

8 minute poem: on being a poet

being a poet
but not a particularly effective
peddler or pimp
I find myself often eschewing
the usual avenues and street corners
to promote myself or my works
more given to the whip of cords approach
at the entrance to the temple

I guess I just have to start dedicating
some time to readings, signings, and appearances
and stop treating the audience
like a necessary evil

(except for the doe-eyed woman in row two
whom I find both necessary and evil
in the better sense of the word)

I don't hate my readers

I am just more comfortable
doing what I do best:

writing in a passion
that borders on religious consummation
and self-immolation.

let's strike a flint
and see if this is holy water or gasoline

barter

the big coin
(immortality)
captured by rapture

if you think you have barter
just up from your garter

some find the notion of
being a muse quite tempting
but you better bring more
than your schoolgirl tricks
to kindle the sparks
and be able to point
to your grandchildren
where you made a mark
resonant in cluttered culture
with romantic fantasies
such that artists and poets
in times to come
try to capture the shape of the scars
you will leave on my satiated soul

Cheshire

the smile you bring is not universal but unique for you,
summoned by your charm and beauty and energies, dark and sweet
like the glaze of a fresh pastry from the oven.
soft and hypnotic, driven to delight and excel,
memories yet to be made and the fading of daylight
turning into a blessed opportunity to be
nothing but a smile, but ever present until…
until you summon me to be more than metaphor
for a goddamn cat, sitting in a tree, contemplating you.

alice

the looking glass never lies
but people do
for their own reasons
from their own ugliness.
tears and the sensation of drowning
in your own fears.
step through
breaking the glass if you must
to find the beauty you fulfill.
then, you will find your way.

Ten million shades of indigo

Ten million shades of indigo
In your eyes, your smile your history and the mystery of what you will discover tomorrow
So much so that I feel blind when I do not contemplate you
When I do not see the world through your eyes,
A constant explosion of jellybean flavors
For the universe is a dull, drab, colorless infinity of grey
Far far beyond black and white
A universe of the undead
Missing the gentle joy of blue morning glories
The intoxicating scent of apricot palinka
The timber of your laugh
And a dream of a dream of a prayer.

the revolution will be digitized and shown on YouTube

the digital renaissance kicked off about 25 years ago
words and images spinning out of control
around the world.
my Panther Cycles have been read on every continent
my poem "A Touch of Heather"
has been banned in a Catholic Girls' High School
in Dundalk, Ireland.
half of the women I have said "I love you" to
in my poetry
are continents away

romance is only part of the whole, though

the essence, the Zen, is communication

mediocrity often, ironically, hidden by sound and fury
and photoshop
in the beginning is the word
in the end is the word
and that still small voice that spoke to Elijah
is still the word on the page
that outlives the theatrics
and sometimes
sometimes
builds a legacy

for poetry, like God,
is not in the wind. the earthquake. the fire.
it is the still small voice
penetrating our minds
our souls
our understanding
with trippingly excellent words and allegories
bent and spent against our defenses and pretenses.

quoted, sugar-coated,
Shelly, Shakespeare, and Byron (my brother in practice)
do not survive their flesh because of a dog and pony show
but because
the words matter.

now we stand on a precipice.
Western civilization teeters and totters and slaughters
shepherds in Afghanistan and black men in Wisconsin
because our bullets hit harder than words
but poetry, like gravity, is a subtle energy
and converts our lovers
our brothers
our sisters
our children
and their children's children's children

into a splinter of the truth we spat out
because we saw the red wheelbarrow
and it invoked a sense of wonder and thunder
within the poet's dreams

rise up. rise up. rise up and let your words unleash
real, true, universal power to elevate the revolution
to power love and pain and guilt and joy
and the occasional memory of things
we wish we'd done or wish we hadn't

tear down the false idols, stand at the barricades
and lead the parades of emancipation
for every black white red brown man woman non-binary
gay transgender bisexual lesbian queer liberal conservative
and spread your mindseed to the world, to the universe
so that even if bad men and madmen
destroy us all and all the planet
one day someone or something will hear your words
and envy us our passions and our truths

Xochiquetzal

your breath is intoxicating evidence that you are alive
and as it quickens it amplifies life to a sacred mystery
to be untangled as we tangle like writhing lithe liars
speaking the truth only with flesh and inner spirits
released in the task caskets of our transfigurations.
Veils sail away in a shower of flowers, butterflies
and the manifold marigolds strewn in your path.

ruby blue and true, blood floods and courses,
forces we cannot deny try as we might to fight the surrender,
pretender to a false immodesty. transcendent precedents
swept from the table as soon as we are able
to catch our breaths and affirm our deaths
in a celebration of a thickening taste we placed
like communion wafers of an intimate religion.

leave no stone unturned, our band and brand is burned
into the cracked and sacked altars stacked high in our inquiry,
our diet of wyrms wherein we throw down our theocricide
ride our preferred angels into the heavens
on until morning becomes another charade parade
of the pretense of civilization we shed last night.

faith healer

pour out your soul in soft sibilance
that I may place hands upon it
and draw the sickly-sweet venom
that has festered deep
within a heart apart from mediocrity.
beauty a curse for drawing things darker than moths
and the casual stare.

I touch without entering,
only to draw into me the virulence
of violence and silence
that has laid pain and stain to strain
your very soul to cry out for healing,
a sealing of the crypt where slipped the past
to make plot against your person.

I touch and feel the soft and subtle warmth
that radiates from within,
a sin of sentience,
trapped in amber to be sapped in agony,
the cold boldness of those who do not
understand or respect the reflection of God within you.
I feel your soul moving in turbulent thought.

I touch and you draw me into you,
no pretender but a tender surrender
of my boundaries to feel the pain you seal
in soft words spoken as dare and prayer
when those you care to let lay hands upon you
are offered a trip to an altar of communion
with an aspect of the religion of avatars of life.

I touch and your sweet sweat
releases the sorrow that flows into my skin,
as I am the conductor of light into dark places
that no one faces alone and survives,
lives fractured every day by those who
play with the tools of the alchemists and amomancers,
faux dancers who lack the grace or experience.

I touch you as you lay upon me,
silent but for a soft breathing,
your leaving not imminent but soon,
for I have done my duty and peeled pain from beauty
to serve the unforgotten gods of love and promise.
my hands can feel you rise and fall in subtler ways
than mere moments before, when transfigured by ecstasy.

last night in paradise

Dance with me, foregoing the artifice,
lovers on the verge of more than a kiss.
The moment made of cream and strawberries.
The pretense-perfect music that carries
an intoxicating rhythm and flow
that supposes that we know what we know
when the mysteries remain on the floor
and the linen cocoon finds nevermore
our vanities, ascendant to great light
transfigured in the darkness of the night.

wasting time and temperament

a second gong sounds in plastic and metal and glass
the roadway littered with sharps and shards
while I clear my head
no one injured
but a familiar process grips me

like that time a lifetime ago
when God had gotten tired of me wasting time
and temperament
slowly sliding out of the darkness
to find the grey way of desperation

waiting for the worms
maybe next time I won't be so lucky
maybe next time
I shall be in the grace of a lover
who gives me reason to pick up my bed and walk

not just talk about the memories of jasmine tea
a sea I sailed upon once for endless nights
when the lights were not brighter but newer
the gong awakes me
to reconsider a life in lower gears

a torn rose petal

a torn rose petal, not by hand of man or woman,
but by the very nature of nature, entropy.
destruction as a creative act. the very fact
that change is not always pretty until you look close
and then from afar, the macroscopic gives context.

God speaks with a voice sub rosa, then subtle, silent!
allowing you mistake your own maelstrom as divine
when you are the shouting village idiot, madness
leading a confederation of ignorant pride,
release your preconceptions and enter the garden.

ronin apocalypsis

there are worse things than being ronin.
exile from the smile and pleasure of the regent
whose very presence defines you, empowers you
such that the brittle kata of the lost warrior
remains only as a shadow, your heart beating
only out of habit. the pain draining you
until the leeches themselves choke on the dust
of a crushed, hushed heart. how long can it beat
when the disembowelment is fait accompli?
I only trust that God will judge with a kinder
disposition my sins, or I am so fucked.

but, I digress, I would express my emotions
with clarity and the charity of one who never lies
or walks away from an accident, even an enemy
deserves the quick kill or a pardon, but I am torn,
worn, scorned and borne, bound and soundless,
into the presence of my own demons, who delight
in the feast release in a single hapless incantation.
better the pen should have fallen from lifeless fingers
than I should face the mockery of my chains.
better I should find penance in all manner of sacrifice
than be cast into exile for the rest of my existence.

BC 1434

the hollow eyes.
lies
and the taste of vinegar.
blades that have slayed
and laid
tracks to the addict's veins.
the remains of city walls
thrown down with the temple.
pain becoming a drug
to dull the doubt
shouting words
unheard
in the chambers
of a nautilus
deep beneath the cold
black waters
of the Pacific
where I sleep
until mourning
my flesh unfit
for the worms.

feigning

feigning sleep when all I could do
was lay awake and dream of you.
your perfect flesh a canvas of desire
a poetry of warm presence, eloquent
and true. beautiful and mesmerizing.
not yet. maybe never. but dreams
are the currency of lovers at night.

the curse of beauty

she was
and is
porn star pretty
more is the pity
the nitty gritty shitty city
grinds that currency up
and hollows it out
boring scoring pouring out hope and joy
like soul-flavored Pixy Stix
onto a greedy receiving tongue
bartering beauty for security
which is a valid choice
as long as the voice making it is hers

The Crown of Sonnets: Mariya

1: eyes of glass

An elegant beauty, eyes of glass and silvered
like visions captured now in a digital age,
caged in frames to lay immortal, white, black or red,
the pale pinks and greys of flesh and fantasy, sage
thoughts unspoken for the thousand-word proxies caught
and projected to distant voyeurs, the silent
partners in a dance of your soul, flying and fraught
with consequence that slips away like a serpent.
You own your dreams, and barter them for ovations
and more material things. This is the nature
of a true artist, remembered after nations
rise and fall and call out to histories, unsure.
Your images, no matter kisses made, tears wept,
mirrors that retain their images, visions kept.

2: visions kept secret and secure

Mirrors that retain their images, visions kept
secret and secure. Dreams erotic and impure
are prayed away, the debris of yesterday swept
into the street and the new petals emerge, sure
that they are the prettiest flower. And they are,
for new life, new tender traces, these are beauty.
Every morning you rise and prize our bright star
as an omen of the promise of a duty
to find your vision in shuttered winks, never far
from yourself. You are more beautiful than the sun,
and yet you know the eclipse, and the night, they are
always part of your world, given but never won.
Day to night and you drink in what was done or said
as forever as light, as night, as earnest bled.

3: Alexandrite

As forever as light, as night, as earnest bled
by shallow, sallow lovers, brittle stone and bone
passing for alexandrite and sapphire, fear fed
the specter of solitude, of being alone.
I shall not desert you. I shall never hurt you
by intention or mention meant to represent
false feelings or facades that promenade in rue
of lost times and past crimes for which we now repent.
I would merge and purge and surge and emerge from you
reborn a better man, to give all that I am,
tribute to all I would ask in simplest hope, true
to your word and kiss and touch against those who damn
me for my love and loyalty, a lost concept
as prayer on the lips of a woman, words wept.

4: Words wept

As prayer on the lips of a woman, words wept.
No miracle, merely a repurposed pilgrim
seeking something more than mediocrity kept
in cold shadows, held in failed light to fade and dim
as a mistaken memory. I want, desire,
an holy fire. As mortal soul may reach for God
I reach for her, with the truth she can inspire
within me, revelation that evens the odd
cobblestones on a path that leads into her heart.
If the divine is in all things, then in my lust
I find sacred blossoming and rebirth part
and sum of my affections, not a graven dust.
I have dreamed of her in scriptures for her to bless.
I have dreamed of her in midnight kiss and caress.

5: Midnight kiss and caress

I have dreamed of her in midnight kiss and caress.
Exotic, the erotic possibilities
beyond my imagination, for tenderness
and urgency merge in a perfect heat, to please
her in sharp moments and sleepless nights, the delights
that would shock satyrs and sate each wish and need
is a command and demand of my passions, flights
of worship of her limbs and form and warm, wet mead
I would consume into a drunken stupor, voice
to brave and wicked utterances in the tongues
of forgotten religions, idolatry's choice
of our histories and mysteries to be sung.
I would be the priest, temple tender to her fires.
I have seen her conquering the world as she requires.

6: Awe

I have seen her conquering the world as she requires.
Small corners taken from the darkness, vast vistas
overcome with the sweep of her hand, she inspires
awe in those capable of perceiving the laws
of a universe she is free to bind to her,
to make bend and flow and go her way, she is strong.
When she believes, she weaves tapestries to ensure
that all memory reflects her perspectives, long
after she is gone, she will linger in the hearts
of those who see the beauty she had seen and caught
in the faery nets of digitized silver, parts
of a mosaic of her laugh and smile and thought.
But not greater than her beauty, I must confess.
Sleek and slender, tender heart my passions to bless.

7: Tender heart my passions to bless

Sleek and slender, tender heart my passions to bless.
Reaching out to God, seeking a permanent peace
with the divine to find the truth and the noblesse
obligation to give of herself a release
to share her heart and soul in a colder world, grey
except when the tulips bloom too rare, too rare to
fill every day with their palette and to stay
as guardians and heralds of joy made anew
every day, every way. Snow is welcome
only for a season, only for a reason
in her street corners and window boxes, made numb
by the cold wind and colder hearts, the freedom
to be seeking sanctuary in her desires.
Holy water, her sweat anoints the sacred fires.

8: Nazarite's hair

Holy water, her sweat anoints the sacred fires.
I would bathe in this purifying sheen, made clean,
the purity of her darkest pleasures, desires
to a purpose and to the moment, visions seen
a thousand times, the cascade of Nazarite's hair
that falls as veil that fails to hide her rare beauty.
Dreams invoked and provoked, words spoken to the air
in hopes that God listens to hopeless prayers, duty
of supplicant and paramour, seeking heaven
in her touch and kiss, to be the missionary
positioned to enter the temple, no heathen,
but believer seeking to merge without tarry.
To be the lover ordained to her dreams and needs.
To be the father of her children, to plant seeds.

9: To plant seeds

To be the father of her children, to plant seeds.
A contemplation and consummation to love.
How many are so blinded by her that their needs
are far simpler. Far less ambitious, nothing of
the need to do more than see her beauty, frozen
in frame and to dream in liquid frustrations, held
at a distance by their own cowardice. Chosen
dreams that objectify her elegant heat, welled
as tears of pale sorrow to their own failed courage.
Delicate derisions and sour grapes to shield
fragile egos, they stare and dare nothing, they rage
and blurt guttersnipe appreciations, revealed
as shadow hearts, daring naught, never to ensure
joy and awe, the law of a prophet transfigured.

10: Transfigured

Joy and awe, the law of a prophet transfigured.
I watch you dance and see the grace of an angel.
The curve and swerve as you move me, so self-assured,
knowing that I must look, caught up as the stars fell.
You became the heavens in my heart long before
I could confess it in manner but clever song.
Your pout shouts and your smile is evidence and more
that there is a God behind the scenes, making wrong
into the kindness of your very existence.
You are worthy of adoration, of a grace
more than most can ever comprehend, persistence
of a melody as ancient as time to place
offerings on the altar to your released needs.
Grace in a place of madness, a sadness that bleeds.

11: In a place of madness

Grace in a place of madness, a sadness that bleeds
pain and stain and the grain of rough roads, the burden
that can take you, break you, make your rosary beads
worn and torn and shorn of meaning. Uncertain
yesterdays and the question of light, bright beacons
or a subtler shade. Draw into sharp relief lines
that define our divinity. Dead eyed deacons
preaching their own religions, never serving wines
of a Holy Land where you stand, an artist's heart
brings forth revelation in the transmutation
of a beautiful woman into icon, part
of a plan to a sensual resurrection.
The vessels of our communion, we are assured,
warm wine and white blood, a soft surrender deferred.

12: Soft surrender deferred

Warm wine and white blood, a soft surrender deferred.
Take me to your bedchamber, I will anoint you with attars
I brought with me from the furthest corners of conscience, cured,
passed through the sunlight and the moonlight and the stars
wise, as my intent is both pure and plutonic,
I am consumed with passion for your bright beauty,
elegant, exceptional, sweet and ironic
that I am captured to pay a perfect duty
as hostage to your murmured sadness and the sweet,
for you are greater than I am, Hephaestus bound
to your Aphrodite, a bold acolyte daring to compete
for that which he could never be worthy, of, found
as foundation to what I most desire this night,
to love the lady with the eyes that capture light.

13: Eyes that capture light

To love the lady with the eyes that capture light.
Now there is a path that I would gladly follow,
happily walking, shadow or rain, day or night.
We are born to love the worthy that fill, hollow,
the center of our souls, where we mislaid the faiths
to believe in perpetual passion and fire
that there are those who can and will dismiss the wraiths
if we let them in with open heart and conspire
with the angels themselves to make a place of peace
where we may dare and share and care to fulfill life
against the hell others wallow in without cease.
We are made to rise above the pain and the strife,
we are made to dance and love and seek for the light,
to dream of memories to be made in the night.

14: Memories to be made in the night

To dream of memories to be made in the night.
To think of you, wrapped around me like second skin,
whispering your most wicked will for the delight
that you will never leave, never allow the sin
of sharing such intimacies with another,
holding nothing back. The hunger and fantasies
that you deserve to fulfill, lady and mother,
courtesan and princess, whatever would most please
your needs and make you but more hungry for my blood,
with smile and kiss and curve of that prehensile tongue,
I will listen for your subtle direction, flood
you with my essence, that all your sweet songs are sung
in my arms, cradled and enabled, my delight:
To dream of memories to be made in the night.

15: The Diadem

An elegant beauty, eyes of glass and silvered
mirrors that retain their images, visions kept
as forever as light, as night, as earnest bled
as prayer on the lips of a woman, words wept.
I have dreamed of her in midnight kiss and caress.
I have seen her conquering the world as she requires.
Sleek and slender, tender heart my passions to bless.
Holy water, her sweat anoints the sacred fires.
To be the father of her children, to plant seeds,
joy and awe, the law of a prophet transfigured,
grace in a place of madness, a sadness that bleeds
warm wine and white blood, a soft surrender deferred.
To love the lady with the eyes that capture light.
To dream of memories to be made in the night.

Thetis had a daughter

So clever and tender Thetis had a daughter
hidden behind a man's name...
as pure and sorrowful as her mother,
smothering her sadness
beneath her studies with Erato.
Obscurant to those who see only with eyes or,
in the case of Polyphemus, eye,
yet can see the truth and sings her songs
of gossamer beauty with vigor and eloquence enough
to wake a slumbering Amomancer
to take up his song and, having seen her
and discovered her true nature,
lady of sorrows, borrowing the bard's cards
to shelter her from the colding winds,
lifts his aged voice to thunder her praise.
The tapestries begin anew their weavings,
mysteries in the histories yet unveiled.

Cracking the Gimcrack Artifices around the Burning Bush

Intro

driven to the brink
we think ourselves competent
competent to contemplate our very nature
nurture future impure and unsure
fragile standing stones
easily corrupted by the tides of history and herstory
our bastard ores melting at varying heats

Transition

the thinnest veneer shades fear from madness
the best beat bestiary hermetically sealed
in congealed wet spots on the satin sheets
where all promises are in the moment

Third Movement

caesurae fury in the darker corners of a sphere
tears that tear the fabric of our perceptions of time
crime to the dreamlords who do not have to wake
breaking dawn unpatched unmatched and thatched
hatches against the rain and stain, memory made
laid across the chasms of orgasms and suffering

Sotto Voce

tinkling tingling bells in the distance, persistence rewarded
with the medium stuffed bear, the big one only for winners
not just dogged effort and sporting propositions, positions
learned from a sideshow slideshow wordplay bloodspray
evidence of our history made in dark rooms when alone
atoning for our solitude in gratuitous gratitude, deep
sharing of our most intimate revelations in nerve endings
electroconvulsive therapy that seals our secrets within

Fifth Movement

the dichotomy of the erotic and the sacred
is not dichotomous. they are one and the same.
blame the Creator whose name we invoke
in goad and overload, flesh becoming metaphor

as our communion is at a higher temperature
and the warm wine is white, aperitif withheld
until after the body is consumed to nourish
the coexistent consecration of lovers' faith

Crescendo

I will look into your eyes if they are open
to enter you on every level possible
there is more to the coit than the copulation
of lip to hip to slip a grip in various orifices
to the solemnification of treasured pleasures
sacred in the religion of poets and lovers
where the transfiguration is replayed
as many times as necessary to your joy

Epilogue

I remember everything, dammit. Everything.
the texture of your lips, the taste of your breath.
the words you whispered then recanted once
it was too late to take them back and stack
your denials against my memory, imperfect
but full of you and the sound you made
as we parted at the airport and you wept
as doubt crept into your heart that there would be
another christening into our generate dreams

foreplay and afterwards: one

the shadows in the room are soft and patient.
not at all like me, as I am waiting for you, now.
I watch you cross the room, dancing on bare feet,
a faint smile of apprehension on lips I will kiss
and violate. first tongue. and then while I
explore your fragrant realms with my lips and fingers,
it will be to you to draw me in and find the pleasure points
that will anoint you with my need and seed
as I feel your body writhe to my touch and trespass.
drink deeply, for the night is just begun
and by morning, we shall be wasted and worn, torn
from the security of who we thought we were
as the lines melted and burned and I yearned
to hear you call my name, one more time, impaled
upon my desire. unlike a boy, my hunger is undiminished
by a single meal, and you feel yourself taken in ways
you did not imagine in your most heated fantasies,
penetrated, desecrated, violated, elevated
and let to fall, limp and helpless as I consume
all that I wish to, your body a chalice of heat.
feel my flesh inside you, gliding through
the channels of your release, your peace
earned in nerves electrified by an ardent tutor
who shares what he has learned that you might,
for one night, feel what you should feel
every night for the rest of your life.

foreplay and afterwards: two

lay back, rest your weary head on pillows
soft and cool. soon enough they will burn
with the pounding blood in your veins.
but for now, lay smooth shoulders back
and slide your fingers into my hair
to guide me, to add another dimension
as my hands part your slender, tender thighs
and my lips kiss scar and pink flesh
going solferino to my attentions
and intentions, as my tongue parts folds
to find entry into you.
my hands, they slide beneath you
pulling you against me as your fingers
twine in my hair, showing me the rhythm
you want me to set as I wet and whet
feasting on your ardent hips and lips.
feel more than hear my moans of delight
as they mingle with your own, your legs
rising to wrap around me as I slide tongue
to tease and please and ultimately
release you to your own need for my touch.
deeper than you know, and yet, not yet,
to ride inside you to the edge of madness.

foreplay and afterwards: trey

I explore your body with fingertip precision,
eyes closed so as not to be distracted as I
find my way along the gentle curves to the nerves
that make you move, like that, and sigh, like that,
and relax enough, just enough, to give me access
to more than soft, warm flesh, but your secrets,
your desires, the fires of your heart and mind
that will burn me before the night is through,
but not before I find how deep you'll let me in.
in metaphor and throbbing, curved shaft that slides
into your sheath, as your senses boil and roil
and your body becomes incandescent to my touch
and trespass. you are tight and warm and wet,
and your arms and legs bind me to you, as if
I could ever imagine wanting to not go deeper
into the labyrinth of your passion and lust.

foreplay and afterwards: quad

lay back, lay back. you need only receive
the hunger of my flesh. spread wings of pink
and solferino and draw me in, skin and sin
passing thin membranes to fetch your desire
and stretch you to the point of a madness
that is the vanity of sanity unburdened.
wrap those legs about me, lock them tight
that I may not go far, mere inches, to return
with shuddering force in the course
of expressing my passions for you.
lay back. lay back. my attack is begun
and the battle is won in its commencement.
I want to feel your hands on my back,
your nails scrailing bloody rivulets
as evidence of your feral essence awakening
and taking me as plutonic as your core.
more of you I measure, treasured pleasures
taking the time it takes to make immolation
a desired, required, inspired poetry of heat
in expressing my passions for you.

foreplay and afterwards: five

be still.
be very still.
listen and feel.
your head, pressed against my chest
finds the rhythm of my heart
matched by the pulse
my pulse
throbbing inside you
every surge of blood
pressing tighter
in an already improbably tight fit.
kiss me.
and when you are ready
move.
slowly at first.
then as you wish
rising up to take full measure
as quickly as you wish
or slow enough to match
the pulse we are sharing
until the barriers melt
and our bodies merge waters
like two rivers meeting
in a roaring turbulence
in which we'll lose ourselves

nightfall angel

at the moment of the gloaming
when the shadows freeze and fade
you will find me waiting for you,
full of passion, unafraid.

as you flit between the willows
and hover, out of reach,
so to lure me by my yearning
to the grove of birch and beech.

where you will drop the pretense
and our clothes shall follow course
as we lay as lovers consummate,
as we plumb this madding source.

you will drain me of my virtue,
you will drain me of my fears,
you will render me a mystery,
drawing out the leper's tears.

I shall hold you while you let me,
and release you when we fade.
I will lay in darkness, bound to you,
e'en if your heart plays charade.

there is nothing here, within me,
I would not let you feast upon,
until I am but memory
and my life and soul are gone.

you are angel in the nighttime
with a light that flickers bright
as you take me for a lover
and consume me with delight.

Queen of Black Hearts

I envy your fingers
subtle stand ins for my touch
and tongue and more
stroking in emphatic rhythm
to feel your legs tense
and wrap around me,
deep inside you. the taste
sweeter than any wine.
the sensations, divine.
the taut, hot tunnel into you
as I kiss your sweet face
and listen to your urgings,
wanting to feel me
deeper
even though it is already
excruciating to have me
fully inside you, your lips
to mine, your breasts
against my chest and you
swallow me up inside you
as I ride you to the edge
of limits of my sanity.
before I swear your name
and lay sharp teeth
to tender flesh
to take my fill in your blood
as you feel me flood
you with my warm, white wine
of surrender as we dance
convulsions of joy and damnation.

Empathy for the Lovers

Movement One: Sonata: The Lovers.

The theology of passion bests the ecology of innocence.
A martyrdom to achieve transcendent life, bound to freedom.
Love. Life beyond life. Immortality in this transcendence.

I am not anyone you have known before, no evidence
exists that I would treat you as they have, where I am from
the theology of passion bests the ecology of innocence.

My words are my music, trouvere of the meme's persistence
that will make of you legend, priestess and queen of my kingdom.
Love. Life beyond life. Immortality in this transcendence.

You have my faith and fealty, my dreams fade my reticence
to leap from high parapet, you are my blood and martyrdom.
The theology of passion bests the ecology of innocence.

Do not mistake my manners or kindness for hesitance,
I am vested in the Gotterdammerung. I am bound to what is to come.
Love. Life beyond life. Immortality in this transcendence.

All issues beyond the ken of any, even the poets' eloquence.
Love is like the ether, even to those deaf to their heart's thrum.
The theology of passion bests the ecology of innocence.
Love. Life beyond life. Immortality in this transcendence.

Movement Two: The Death of Illusions

The theology of passion. A bold assertion,
that affections and lust might be a religion,
Aphrodite and Venus and Jesus spun into a cloth
of conflicting aspect. Catching the light in reds
both crimson and scarlet. Purifying and a branding
of sin and sanity, the vanity of daring to love.
I have faith in love, if not the lovers,
for we are frail and fail to fulfill the tale
we told ourselves in bolder times of hope.
The rope runs short and our feet still dangle,
with no way to see how far the fall but to let go
and risk everything. Even our belief in those
we chose to love, unlacing the traces to let fly
with wings of amber and of fire, graceful lies
unwound as the ground falls away and we play
at the phoenix. We make our own legends.
Fallen angels. Risen prophets. And the space between
the hallowed hollowing of our hearts to make room
for the opportunity of a real moment. Patience.
There is virtue in the long painful climb of the hill
where we know our persecutors would kill us
to prove nothing but their own powers.
And yet, love abides, resides and provides
a portal into the immortal wilderness of the soul.

Movement Three: Lyrical Variations on a Dream

Love. Life beyond life. Immortality in this transcendence.
In this world we are curled around our own cores.

Fear is the great disabler. Fear of loss. Of gain. Of the stain
of blood and more fel fluids that we drip out, rip out
in moments of surrender, pretending nothing for the instant
when tears are shed by more than eyes. Making a connection
in more than affection and drunken fumblings, stumbling
up the stairway to the altar when we are to be sacrificed
into our own deification. Releasing into one another.
The solitary soul is an illusion. A starving man eats anything
he can get his hands on and dies, poisoned with a full belly.
I want to see you sated in and with this life, wife to contentment.
You are like fractured gems set in the night sky, illuminated
by a mythology we ourselves wrote and sugar-coat
when all along we nod at the pain we will still have to endure.
The purity of you is in your darkest doubts. I have them, too,
but I have spent too long on the battlefield to accept
the conqueror wyrm as my better. I will kiss your scars
when the stars are aligned in keeping with your prophecies.

Movement Four: The Chaos of Erotic Innocence

Tears are wept. Promises kept except those to ourselves.
A final muse, a tacit refusal to embrace, for now, a future
with only a few certainties, for we are not yet there.
Care if you can, dare if you must, trust what is proven.
We need not play this game so badly or madly, sadly
we have proven ourselves from time to time, incompetent.
I have only faith to support my suppositions, not a thread
of a promised sackcloth and vestment has been offered
without being snatched back by the black hand of fear.
I am here, I am near, it is clear I would not make this walk,
speak this talk, dare your mockery if I was not sincere.
I have wandered the world to find you, and to be kind to you.

We are reborn in the shadow of our own illuminations.
Innocence suffuses us as a choice, a voice of passion
that we can fashion into whatever we want to taunt
the fates that so often have left us, broken and bleeding,
needing more than the nothing we discovered,
but could not bring ourselves to disavow because
we thought pride would protect us, direct us to something,
something more than the dust of lust tasted and wasted
because we couldn't wait for the banquet being prepared
for us in the presence of the enemies of our ascensions.
The chalices of change arrange themselves left to right,
each brew made only for our lips, our tongues, our nourishment.

The smallest sip that touches the lips of my love, I taste.
Cut and pasted to the tapestry. Not out of weakness,
for I can bend the very winds to my command if needs be,
but because I have taken a solemn vow and am damned
beyond this life if I break it, not to the whim of a deity,
but to my own memory of perfidy and the tyranny
of pale poisons let into the wedding cup. I acknowledge
that I may stand alone at the end, my passionate friend
having deserted me for less perfect purposes, and this as well
is a definition of Hell, to live out my hours, days and years
with only the screaming winds, drawing from me every thought,
caught in the maelstrom, as company, as I slowly fade.

I would not be changed for the experience, for my love
will remain, in my words and memories and my blistered heart,
beating on until it can no longer find time to bend, to spend
in an eternal passion for you. There are those who would
consider this a wasted life, but we are not measured by love
that comes to us, but by the love we give, unconditionally
and freely, praying in silent corners that our words are heard
and are palatable enough to feed the needs of our paramour.
It is a hard conceit, to walk the line between the divine
and the defiled, seeking subtle seduction through true words.
But anything more or less would be disrespectful of you,
and if I did not feel such awe I would not dare to love.

orphan

collect me. respect me. protect me.
for I am alone in this world.
hurled from care and comfort.
bare feet and broken heart are parts
of the whole that means something.
something I feel but cannot express
except in sad sounds and a look
like a fallen angel, seeking solace.
detect me. select me. perfect me.
there must be something wrong with me
that I am outcast and alone, the stone
the builders had no use for, silent
with the violent sorrows of apprehension
that becomes a worldview, untrue,
but easily embraced when you are alone
and all that fit and felt right has fallen.
connect me. affect me. suspect me.

pounce

you regard me as a meal.
perhaps nothing more.
or even just a pleasant scent,
like apple pie, cooling on the sill after baking,
when you know you are on a diet
or it isn't your pie to have
or you are just not in the mood
for the sweet stickiness
with the crumbling crust.
I feel your eyes more than see them.
before my defenses can react
you are behind them,
inside me,
prying loose secrets and confessions
that make you smile,
make you smirk with the knowledge
that you have found
the soft underbelly of my soul.
and the only question lingers.
the only question lingers
is what you will do with me,
now that you have pinned me to the dry grass
and torn me open
without any more effort than existing...

like a lost soul in a cathedral

I should like sometime
sometime
to be there when you wake
and see the skies realize
they have been counterfeiting blue
compared to your eyes.

To watch you stretch
and hear you sigh as light trespasses
across your face
your neck your breasts
and lends warmth to make the morning
more palatable.

I should like sometime
sometime
to see you pad away to find breakfast
even if it is only a casual thing
with no real nutrition
just you, waking, taking time.

You would be so very
so very
beautiful that I would be silent
like a lost soul in a cathedral
and smile to myself at my redemption.

I should like sometime
sometime
to wake up next to you and ask
myself if this is real or if
I died last night and you are my God.

Villanelle: love

how can a man know a mother's glow, a baby to her breast?
and what of all the lovers who are bent and burnt and scorned?
how can the faithless understand the pilgrim on his quest?
this life is but a puzzle, putting our best to the test,
questions open eyes and lies when our broken hearts are mourned.
how can a man know a mother's glow, a baby to her breast?
we orient to find the way, our destinies lie West.
we'll find our way in brightest day and coldest night reborn'd.
how can the faithless understand the pilgrim on his quest?
I have laid with more illusions than I would count, confessed.
I've elevated doxies, proxies and the nemicorned.
how can a man know a mother's glow, a baby to her breast?
the priceless princesses of earth forswear this graceless test.
but I'm set free when truth I see, my head yet unadorned.
how can the faithless understand the pilgrim on his quest?
the sacrifice is not taken if it is not the best.
love is still the only answer, false prophets all be warned.
how can a man know a mother's glow, a baby to her breast?
how can the faithless understand the pilgrim on his quest?

April 2016: a cycle of life

on the nature of poets

I once tasted a petal of clover, but that does not make me a honeybee,
merely a curious seeker unable to restrain myself from the moment
where I could imitate, faintly, the actions of the bee, aping the apis
to try to understand from where comes the honey, the nectar.
it was revelatory as the scale of the essence I partook of shook free
the magnitudes of mortal man from insect. imitation by rote of role
constrained by nature and the Almighty is not the same as transfiguration.
I am not the clover. not the honeybee. I draw my sustenance in inspiration.

the undodged curtain (for my Mother)

I did not watch them shovel the rude earth over your mortal remains.
for that is not how I would remember you, celebrate you.
how many times had you dodged the curtain? more than I knew, no doubt.
but it comes to this, a separation of mother and children
by the very ground we walked upon just weeks ago,
laying flowers on my Father's grave you now lay beside.

to an eager lover's religion

brighter than the fractured morning. she calls me with her kisses.
too far away to feel then, to savour her breath or the texture
of her moist lips, slipping into a transcendental trance to dance
across my skin and soul like faerie in the absinthe, green and greedy.
I am ready for the rapture, theologically or held within her.
worshipping as an earnest acolyte to the delight of the night
when she sheds clothing in a disarray, like a torn veil in the temple
where all mysteries are to be revealed to the patient pilgrim.

a soft pink ghost upon the wall inside my skull

I thought of you and all the promises you meant at the time you made them.
I admit, I still miss you, kiss you in dreams heated and sweet, holding nothing back
as I embrace the blackened corners that are foreign to me, for you are not there,
merely a simulacrum of your beauty, your fire, the feral desire that was light without heat,
bone without meat, even when cracked open for the marrow in desperation.

biscuits

the rain reminds us all that we do not
control even the soft fall of heavens.
it speaks to us words of a held tongue, caught
expressionless, yet eloquent, leavens
the pale and dry biscuits of our conceits:
powder and salt and lard, concealing taste
only in the baker's skills, the bland treats
seeming as more unto punishment, waste
of our attentions and intentions. lips
split and bloody as our cursed thirst damning
to a revelation of lives' eclipse
as we watch the kitchen timer turning,
mysterious clockwork and alchemy,
our lives measured by hands we cannot see.

measuring disaster in decibels of laughter

measuring the steps to the ledge, then running to turn
and leap
and fall
with practiced panic and the graceful disgrace
that saves face in the last instant and inches
before disfigurement and death
the breath of god and the occasional kind goddess
giving life at unexpected instants and instances
dances of the dreamers
that I will am still able to perform
even in my hermitage and hermit's age.

when all is sad and done

will you stay with me
will you lay with me
until all is sad and done
and the sun reconsiders rising
for just an instant
out respect

when I leave
will you grieve
briefly
then remember
that I was about celebration
and dance barefoot on the kitchen floor

Playing the hard Abelard in the Game of Hearts

I.

I fold, cold, cards rough to my fingers.
the bitter and brittle fear rising like vomit
in my throat, coating me in a mist of mysteries.
histories echoing with every doubt, case out.
road kill in the still morning air, food for fortune.
instinct blinking out with final thready heartbeats.

II.

at a distance puppets dance mad and sad,
our taint restrains tensions tested to wrest
incidental assumptions now made mad
as they burrow deeper to at length best
well-wrought defense, made of memories won
in games of chance with cards cut from our flesh
to bear barter for hearts in grimmest fun
mocking our marks, wagers we can refresh
from the seeming endless Tantalus purses
we hide, inside, to bide time for the tell
presumed in eyes that lie out of curses
ancient as an holy scripture, God's spell
cast in castrations of divinity
as we take hemlock from necessity.

III.

the shadows dance because the fire does
and so do we
and our chaotic nature does not permit us
vision of all elements at once
so we play the dunce
understanding that control is an illusion

IIII.

the lion holds his wrath
because, somehow, he feels
that it is not the antelope's fault
that it was born without claws
or jaws enough to make a worthy prey

V.

the Apollonian balance blanches at the excesses
of demons chained and near starved in old stone.
encrypted like the black words they spit
in a tongue I alone know the Rosetta stone.
hard and near permanent, illuminated
scripture to a mad God's religion, sacrifices
proving only desperation and not worthiness.
I spit blood then split atoms, then start again,
the formula for the ritual not yet perfected.

VI.

the invitation is given.
no one accepts.
the temple is emptied
and the cycle begins again.
the religion is in the teachings.
but a God without worshippers
will slowly fade to legend.
then, into nothingness.

VII.

upon fresh stones and the attar of roses
I contemplate my cithara
then seek a new pluck of the strings
to bring perhaps a new magic
a summoning of something new
something
something less uncertain
still, in my stubbornness
refusing to surrender to doubt
in the eventual outcome
the elegance of sacrifice
the beauty of love
in a world of fragile, shattered prayers

Torn and Tossed

Torn and tossed, a Pentecost of more than five dimensions.
Slow to break the fast that lasted half a step of the dance
and then some. Kisses in scarlet and solferino, memory runs
and locks itself away. Playing for time expended in chance
opportunities that pleased all and none depending on the filter
of the perspective through eyes closed in a repose I once chose,
not knowing the price of commitment to the greater good, impure
like a diamond, to a first water. Last man out as the second sun rose
to bring a light that castrates the night but only for a season
or a score of seasonings, reasonings resounding in a pounding
like an elusive heart that has finally found the tempest tapestry, reason
enough to wait for the late fate of the sound of a heart, resounding.
Lay with me when you are ready, I am in no hurry to waste a resurrection
on the muddied middle of the hymns to a flawed law of perfection.

nails into wood

nails into wood
nails into flesh
the strangest meetings made to mesh
in pain and regret, the stain of a sweat
beyond prophecies and made mysteries.
the deserts fade
the deserts fail
to break the spirit of a dream that doesn't pale
next to the cold shroud, the veil of a cloud
that now will descend a faith to defend.
we bend our will
we bend our whim
and find that we are mere mortals against daemons grim
that make us believe and forget to receive
a sacrament taste of a lover displaced.

roll away the stone

roll away the stone. the stone that seals just one perspective.
for while the flesh is bound by walls and time, I've slipped free
to be a thing of light and quanta, bouncing through the ether
to both send and be a message, in and of myself, as such.
much to relate and yet can anyone relate to the inexplicable
except where a touch or glance communicates subtler truths
than all the hand-wringing head-shaking games when we must
filter reality through the lying layers of the necessity of survival.
the soothsayers and naysayers and game players protest.
too much. hiding from the hidden. forbidden mockeries spilt
like a glass of Pesach wine, long forgotten but the stain remains
for the celebrants to discover years from now, contemplating
what it is and what it means and if blood is really that red.

White as illusions

White as illusions, cast to shade scarlet and crimson
and the black of the human heart in better lights,
transcendent nights where the perfectibility of a kiss
becomes a sexorcism that banishes demons of clay and brass,
glass spiders in graven images imagined to be more
than they were less of, more than what they were,
and of a substance hammered by the artisans
who knew well their craft as they laughed
at their own cunning, running rings around Saturn
and laying myth to the Achilles Heel
of the lost worshipers of polytheism.
A communion of stones and water,
bones that slaughter even after the flesh fails
and the evangelist sails for a purer night
than offered as sacred sacrifice to fallen idols.
How long can you pray to the failed, the scrawled words
on tablets of earth and bone, the deeper demons remain
and the pain is inhuman, put aside for a time to come.

you are a lantern to my soul

you are a lantern to my soul,
lambent to my touch. your surrender
awakens me to make sacrifice
after sacrifice, pieces of myself
given as evidence of a new communion.
the old idols fade and crumble
into piles of dust and sand.
nothing can stand the test of time
but that which is willing to wait.
wait until the time for idols is passed
and we cast ourselves in images
of our true selves, severed from lies
that we even tell to the mirror
to make clearer the falsehoods
we feed upon. I have no need of riddles.
the religion of ronins is patience
and the desire to see things as they are.
I should like to see you naked,
with nothing between us but hope.

a legend perhaps given

a revelation perhaps given before the moon rises.
too soon for the civilization to wrap its soul around.
inconvenience in a thunder clap from out of everywhere.
truth surprises and tantalizes at times most inopportune
but bearing kairos over chronos, time enough for riddles
told in a practiced measure. the rituals of passion
stripped of the sacrament of true spirituality.
flesh to bread. blood to wine. a sense of the divine
in the taste of the sacrifice, given willingly.
cold stone idols and the shadow of the sun passes
into another night, where the chill fill us with doubt
we smother in platitudes and quotations. poster logic
without an understanding of the words, the whimsy,
the amomancy of the brave, slave to nothing,
but bound to speak of small words, sighed and undenied,
inscriptions on warm flesh, to be kissed, drawing out.
water from stone. wine from water. blood from wine.
and the cycle closes with a prayer shared between lovers
and the belief that they have found faith in the night.

memory fails me

memory fails me
at the altar where I kneel
my sins confound me
a past I can not conceal

there are angels in the air
without a thought without a care
and those of us of human form
must trade our souls to be kept warm

the visions recede
the incense precedes

and we are left to dance for hours that stretch to years

our passions resist
and then they persist

and we are left to pray to idols stacked like Russian dolls

you are lovely
and I cannot help but speak
words of yearning
the dream is strong, the dreamer weak

prayer is not wasted on your soul

prayer
is not wasted on your soul
pain
that tried to wrest from you control

of all my fervent promises unbound
in all the sacred travesties I'd found

blood
becomes proof of truth and light
touch
that communicates the night

in all the eloquences I must speak
in the moments before I become too weak

kiss
with a purpose and release
dream
and may you find love and joy and peace

like an ancient elder serpent god

like an ancient elder serpent god
avatar of a darker spirit
slithering up from out of shadows
scale on cool stone, voice like the winds
passing through the drying grass
where once grew trees of life and light.

like a darker priestess, summoning,
waiting for the red and black to melt
and run together like blood and night
the knife left buried, deep and silent,
the violent path to penetrate a heart
no longer of value as you evolve

like fire in the depths of an ancient fen
where no one claims the spark that set
the moss and dead twigs to crackle
like the cackle of creatures in the black.
like the taste of lips and lilacs, warm,
the promise of a ritual of ragged passion

The prison is inside

The prison is inside, we hide our hearts
that none may break them. Pretty venoms spit,
hit their mark, but we are strong for our parts
and bind ourselves in bright rags that are split
only for pretense, we are not naive
to the purposes of tender tensions,
but we choose to guard that which we believe
essential, saving pretty pretensions
for the kiss and coit of those we can drain
for our nourishment and inspiration.
Leaving not death, but life and light, the pain
sucked in the instant of immolation.
I draw from you a flood of blood, a feast,
I share with you a thousand beasts, released.

let slip my leash

let slip my leash and I will run
run with limbs of quicksilver and skin of glass
passing the wind in my flight
laughing at the sun as I bring the night
not the darkness
but the beauty of the night
the song of the stars
the perfume of the moon
the sound of crickets and distant fading winds
as they shake the sleepy trees

I will run to you, eyes full of wonder and thunder,
seeking only to spend what time you allow
padding along the darker paths
to feel the heat of your skin
when you lay to rest
to smell your breath as you sleep
and imagine kisses I would never dare
as I wait for the rising sun
and run back into dreams
where I will await my reward

Nothing good can come of this

Nothing good can come of this.
Nothing good at all.
I feel you pierce my shadowed bliss.
Now in my sunken hall.
You've overrun the battlements
where I had made my stand.
And now cut deep inside my stones
I'd marked with sacred brand.
You're everywhere at once, and yet,
you dance, you dance away.
You've toppled walls in sacred halls,
you drive my thoughts astray.
And what would you, my conqueror,
demand to ransom back
my sanity, my vanity,
my soul on which you snack?
Benign malevolence you are
and beautiful, beside.
You've broken my defenses, token,
and in my heart, abide.

The baptism of desire

The baptism of desire, the fire burns away the doubt and shame.
Risen, like the phoenix, in heat and light and a solferino flame.
Passion descends on you, enters you, pure in its own right, no carnival
can drive away this mystery of the touch, avatars of the carnal
gods reborn to taste with lips and hips the eclipse of bartered ad val,
the baptism of desire, the fire burns away the doubt and shame.
I feel your tempested breath upon me, until nothing but you could tame
the lion of my loins that drives deep to fulfill an ancient aim and claim.
Passion descends on you, enters you, pure in its own right, no carnival
to bid farewell the flesh that meshes in urgent, ardent and unsubtle
stroke and writhe and kiss and rage and the poetry of the deeper thrall.
The baptism of desire, the fire burns away the doubt and shame.
I would gladly die tween the thighs that wrap and slap me, with a poet's name,
taking me for what I am, I surrender my urgent thirst and proclaim!
Passion descends on you, enters you, pure in its own right, no carnival
for I am not to surrender my coeur rage for you, but in you, the same
as you will lay upon my flesh the consecration of your sacred scrawl:
The baptism of desire, the fire burns away the doubt and shame.
Passion descends on you, enters you, pure in its own right, no carnival

the curve of your hip

the curve of your hip
warmer than I expected

my hands trace your body
your grace even in repose
waking in me the songs

have I become an altar
to passions or is it you
or are we sharing brisance
without over-thinking it all

I can smell the heat of you
the sweet wet taste of jasmine
that I have been greedy for

discovering a goddess
in the way you move your hips

would you be among the witness

would you be among the witness
who see me off the edge
daring all to choose to risk the fall
on a lover's boldest pledge?

would you read the tattered journals
and the scripture of my fate
choosing love above the cowardice
that is born in barren hate?

I am not here to ask you anything
but to speak my mind and leave
I have nothing to make offering
never tasking you to grieve

I am just a wandering minstrel
who is not afraid to lose
speaking of the errant arrogance
in whom, for love, I choose.

touch and taste and sound and sight and scent

touch and taste and sound and sight and scent
the veil is rent
and senses flood like blood from a wound
but this warm fluid is not red
not yet
but wet and pulsing life
of a sweeter degree
communicating your desire
your fire
as you kiss fingertips
with lips
thirsty
hungry
trembling to speak
to seek to express
the senses overtaken
with a simple kiss
or stroke of hand
or fingertip
or eloquent tongue
silently making love
that you may find me on more than a page
that becomes my cage
when it is locked away
in rooms you only come to
when you are alone
and you want to feel
your senses light up like a pyre
of dried exotic woods
that you can dance in the light
naked
in flesh and metaphor
grateful for my lips
fingertips
the truth they speak
that you are beautiful
worthy of reverence
and all the deity I need
for my faith to be restored

I want to hear your spirit

I want to hear your spirit
softly calling me
your veins throbbing at the memory
of my touch and trespass

I want to be your addiction
your nasty little habit
that you'd barter your dignity for
your life for an afternoon
with me pumping through your veins
messing with your mind
flooding your blood
dancing in your trance

I am here, whispering your name
a mantra of possession
a sinister confession
that I want to be wanted

will you lay upon the altar

will you lay upon the altar
and offer me your soul
just to see if I will snatch it
in a flash of lost control

will you touch me with desire
that is ancient and anew
draw me in to share your pleasure
a hunger, pure and true

will you dare be my redemption
for my arrogance and fall
that I might yet deserve to set
my compass to your call

will you lay upon the altar
and offer me your soul
just to see if I will snatch it
in a flash of lost control

white

white
white as snow as clouds as dreams
as a puff of smoke
purified by your perfect kiss

white
white as light as milk as frost
as the milkweed seeds
scattered like random thoughts

white
white as bread as bleach as rage
as a blank paper page
waiting on you to compromise its virtue

I heard it

I heard it. The sound of silence cracking around the edge
where the sedge has withered, all dithering aside,
I slide into to momentary gap between words
and find myself absurdly off balance, like a buffoon
in a Renaissance morality play, caught in the act
of acting like a normal human being, a role I am
rare to fill. expectations being what they are
and every scar has a name and a story
that rides with it to the place where the ancient
stop aging and become, themselves, memory.

You are beautiful. And brave and passionate.
and I am not a polished stone, fresh plucked
from the shore to show to friends with glee.
I am driftwood of an intriguing gnarl, you are
an unique flower of a tree I had never encountered
before I caught your scent, all jasmine and spice,
like a pear warmed on a very hot day in August.
I reach to touch your skin and crave to taste you,
your juices sweet and savoury to a familiar tongue.
And I wonder on the nature of wine and desire.

if I lay my offerings at your feet

if I lay my offerings at your feet
would you, at least, consider them?
or would it be a sure defeat
to kneel and kiss your vestment's hem?
questions asked and answered yet,
I have. in past times, failed the test
where my sure heart was given, set
on goddesses who swore in jest.

There are angels and demons

There are angels and demons, creatures of perfect beauty and vile affections.
Then, there is you. Faint taint notwithstanding, it adds to your charms
and I find no harm in having a healthy curiosity and a desire for pleasure.
Indeed, I look forward to when skin meets skin and the thin protections
of our civilized illusions melt like tears before kisses, in my arms
I would find you no less beautiful and perfect, measure for measure
a treasure of your heart, I hope, manifested in more carnal expressions
that we can share with purpose to an expression and consummation, warms
to heat to fire to immolation, in which I would lay suttee, to blend my fate with yours.

I shall make of your flesh a living scripture

I shall make of your flesh a living scripture of Psalms
of love, silencing Solomon and raising a new religion,
bound by passion and earnest sharing of brave hearts.
Fire and light, the taste of you like roses and jasmine,
the way you hold me in sacramental sacrifice, sacred
as any prayer as you dare me to touch corners veiled
by your need to bleed in colours for which there are no words.
I have heard your chants and mantras, prepared a feast
in your name as I lay my hands upon the altar and draw
the very venoms I have tasted in lesser vessels,
vinegar and dregs of oils spoiled in mockery of joy.
What do the dead know of life? What do the silent
know of the sounds made when souls surrender to faith?
Consecrate me and I will lay a seed in the loins of memory.

will you fade away when I come to stay

will you fade away when I come to stay,
will you find a reason to deny me?
I have stepped up and out and far away
from the reassuring stones beneath me.

that I want you is transparent to me
and to all who read my poems and prayer.
that I want you is a miracle to see,
an unexpected corner of life, faerie and fair.

will you fade away when I come to stay,
will you find a reason to deny me?
I have stepped up and out and far away
from the reassuring stones beneath me.

more than a moment

more than a moment.
more than a kiss.
more than forever,
a prayer for you, this.

more than a meeting.
more than a smile.
more than a merging,
purging all guile.

would you come in the moonlight
daring all to the chance
to encompass the twilight
with a dance, a romance
that defies all the logic
and all of your doubt,
that belies all our histories,
the mysteries, cast out.

more than a dreaming.
more than a night.
more than a mem'ry
of exquisite delight

more than is given.
more to receive.
more than you ever
have dared to believe.

This is my Pentecost

This is my Pentecost. Not in chronos, but kairos.
This is important. This. You. How the pieces fit,
not in the force-them-in-and-we'll-work-it-out-later way
that so many people can live with, but how they fall
together. Effortlessly, for now. No doubt there will be
times ahead where things tilt a bit like everything does
or even we find the tunnel of love is a corkscrew.
But if we ride the moment and trust, just enough,
we'll be fine, like lemon wine. I need this kiss.
I need to see you dance once more, barefoot,
catching my whim and will as I imagine centering
myself in the way you move your graceful hips,
trusting your lips don't lie in word or parting
to slide breath between us. Cinnamon dust
and the morning light, a rose on a silver tray,
the way things are supposed to be if we believe.
Grieving over lost and caustic causes, pauses
in the slipstream of the wind of Icarus.
You will find me. Bind me. Grind me.
But in the end I will say it was you who defined me.
For that is the ultimate purpose of a Pentecost.

miracle

miracle.
anomaly.
a strong longing for something,
someone,
from an unexpected corner.
the taste of lace,
fingertips,
wet and whetting an appetite
for tight places
and faces
that will touch with silent eloquence.
and we will be
transfigured.
remade.
a sacrament of flesh and blood
shared
as a celebration of our own
testament
to a new state of being.

take me into you

take me into you. your body a metaphor
for your heart. your soul. the heat
of your body, swallowing me up until
I spill life itself into you, lost to me
forever, but given with great joy and faith.
there is a mystery here, a beautiful
mystery as you feel me moving inside you,
taste yourself on my lips, hold with hands
my body, pressed into you to make us
an evolution of passion and surrender.
no pretender here, just your radiant skin,
drawing me in and wrapping about me.
taking me for your own. making me your own.
an allegory for our spirits, wet and afire.
I will surrender to you all you want, and more,
if only you will bless me with the sacrament
of your body as a parable, a testament, of your love.

your sorrows are my sorrows

your sorrows are my sorrows
your pain, mine own.
I will lay between the rocks and you
and keep you safe, and warm.

I will give you the best I have to give,
leaving no thorns in the flowers I bring.
I will learn to eat what you eat
and never make you listen when I sing.

I will lay beside you when you need me
and I will carry our load when you are weak.
I will listen when you when what is important
or even not, is what you speak.

I will bring you herbs fresh from the meadows.
I will kiss your lips, and yours alone.
I will make this life what I can make of heaven,
and never leave you, never alone.

You beg the trespass

You beg the trespass, steal the crown.
Lips of peaches, ripened to red,
you dare to wear the crimson gown.
To draw out venom from your bed,
power claimed in the pleasured art.
Now courtesan and queen, priestess,
coeur rage born in a battered heart.
And paramour, the idols press
and are shattered in your embrace.
Wondering when and where you've gone,
Helen stares into empty space.
The unexpected quarter, on
past the Pillars of Hercules.
Our fires burn in four degrees.

I surrender my will

I surrender my will, seeking yet more
than mere arrogant posturing, the touch
of the divine. Shackles of pain are poor
purpose in the heavens' mystery, much
remains to be experienced. The sight,
God in the grace of creation, your heart,
manifesting transfiguration's light.
The power of love echoing to part
the seas of the tears and fearful distrust
built on the coward's easy perfidy.
I would merge with your divine, kick the dust
and find the most remarkable beauty:
You as angel and the evangelist
seeks only for the blessing to persist.

What shall be our witness tree

What shall be our witness tree,
our silent witness to our vows?
Where lovers come to speak their hearts
as we did, long before they came.

Perhaps a pine, so tall and straight,
evergreen steadfast symbol.
Catching the odd snow in winter,
keeping live the promise of life.

Perhaps an ancient oak, so strong,
Atlas to the forest sky, true
and earnest, indestructible
next to the frail neighboring boughs.

Perhaps a magnolia, sweet
and heady, refreshing the wind
and flowering to welcome life
and all its possibilities.

They are all witness to us, here,
in the silence of the forest,
where we speak words to God alone
and to one another, our hearts.

I feel the sky

I feel the sky. it weeps for lovers, lost, never
having the opportunity that we have found
to lay down the tepid temptations and sever
heart from flesh, to be woven together and bound
to one another. into a single thing, heal
and seal and feel the pulse of my life inside you.
as I will feel you, fit in me, cast to reveal
all that is worthy, all that is, within you, true.
not the platitudes of rude suitors, seeking spark
but not fire. seeking an abstraction of you,
but never the woman, the child, the bright and dark
angel now woven into me, so very few
are given such surrender into victory.
and the sky no longer needs weep for you or me.

take you the sacrament of my white wine

take you the sacrament of my white wine.
draw out the essence of my surrender,
swallowing my issue of the divine,
your reverence and severance, tender,
from the false religions, idolatry.
old passions pass away, your fingers play
and your warm, hungry mouth tears my flesh free,
the white blood of creation, a wine. I lay
hungry for redemption, tithe of pleasure.
for now, soft pink lips draw tight about me,
tongue, eloquently silent as you measure,
feed and bleed me of all resistance, free
of all free will, your temptation, tender,
witness of your wish to grant me heaven.

there are religions

there are religions, ancient and new,
that do not stir the soul as much as you
stir mine. the essence of your spirit,
the mettle of your soul, near it
I am pulled into the gravity of joy
and can do little but fall, destroy
me with but a single artifice
if you want to see my bliss
turned to tormented desolation.
but know you, my passion,
my affection, is as real as the sun,
and as radiant and heated, won
by nothing more than your being
the revelation I am, in your words, seeing.

for you I want to heal the wounds

for you
I want to heal the wounds
and end the pain
the doubt
the questions that are irrelevant

ten thousand reasons
exist why we don't make sense
ten thousand more
rise to match the impertinence
of anyone
who says love doesn't matter

it does
and can move mountains and part seas
and make the skies light at night.

for you
I want to say the things I have never dared
and share everything i have ever shared
and all because
and all because
and all because
for you
I was put into this world

you may rest here

you may rest here
if you like
if you are weary

I will stand
sentinel to your heart
and your soul

letting no thing
no one
trouble you

my arms will
press you
to me

my heart
will play rhythm
to your breathing
as you sleep

burrowed in
like a kitten
in a blanket

I am warm
and gentle
and mean no harm

I will lay here
and hold you
until mourning comes

if God is God

if God is God should it matter
if we care more for them
than they for us

for there are ten billion
people in the world
and only one God

we need only love one God
(who is confessedly
a jealous God, anyway)

but if we accept the divine
as divine and limitless
how can we hold God faithful?

it is a question for those
greater than me and wiser
for I have so much love I ache

love for everyone, everyone,
but a special sense of love
for the one, jealous God

I am here for you

I am here for you, and yet for my needs.
Greedy and hungry, thirsty for love that
bursts on the tongue like raspberries, the seeds
and juice filling your mouth, no weak or flat
notes in this symphony. Power rises
and rafters rattle, for there is no place
for mediocrity when disguises
are discarded like impudent clothes, face
to face we stand, even at a distance,
reaching for one another to so yield
our essences and crack the resistance
that has, for too long, been a crust and shield
against love as real as would burn heaven
when we give ourselves to transcend our ken.

I'm for trading my memories

I'm for trading my memories for dreams.
You have taken me, awakened me and
I am not desirous of a return, seems
that I am ready to move on to stand
proactive in a last-year world. You plant
hope in me. Hope and firecracker lust,
desire and passion kindled to raise chant
to liturgy. I want to conquer dust
and damnation for your grace, your face,
for every trace of all you have offered
in evocation and prophecy, trace
the tears and tenderness proffered
in acknowledgment that there is something
real and worthy and beautiful coming.

will you close your eyes

will you close your eyes
the first time we kiss
and let all that you are and know
flow into me as I melt into you
my hands sliding down and peeling
your fabric armour
so that we may begin and continue
what we will continue and not finish
for many, many years
if ever?

You shivered in the cold

You shivered at the cold and thought the room
would be empty on your return, iron
headboard still cold and hard and your bridegroom
gone, a sea of insecurities, dawn
and midnight, stolen in a promised kiss
that would never come. But I kept faith, held
on when silence roared for I would not miss
this consecration for life or withheld
my love for doubt. You will always find me,
patient if not perfect. Not only skin
but lambent determination to see
this through with you, to everyday begin
the best I know how, in your heart and arms,
and surrendered to your brave love and charms.

eyes that do not beg the greater question

eyes that do not beg the greater question
but ask with gentle reproach to be given
a moment's, an hour's, a night's release
and peace from the sorrowful shallows of life.
skin, soft and taut, warm to the touch.
lips like rose petals, soft and full of life.
breasts, flawlessly risen to pink meringues
that demand a taste so as not to waste
the beauty of their pleasant presence.
thighs, lean and inviting, more than a night
on white satin, calling soundlessly the lover.
the feast is spread and the bed the canvas
to the work of the art and religion of surrender.

I will blossom to your touch

I will blossom to your touch.
grey bark falling away.
my limbs rising to seize once more the heavens
and wring out the tears of angels
in the name of love they cannot know,
for it is but for the rare mortals
and the small gods.

I will blossom to your touch.
new roots laying in, deep,
anchoring me to you, my Earth and Venus and sky.
you are the gentle magic of my life
and I will draw my beauty, every petal
and leaf and limb, from your dreams
and share with you.

I will blossom to your touch.
I will find my way to you.
I will place myself in a convenient corner and grow
until I am the source of the shade
until I am the tree of your life
until I am the bearer of fruit
until I am gone.

damn you for awakening me

damn you for awakening me.
I had slept longer than I had dreamt possible
and had accepted my fate as a sleep unto death
but you walked in and with a single kiss blew breath
into these grey and shriveled lungs. I feel life.
I am alive.
my heart, no longer merely beating because it can,
hammers within my breast with the fury of creation,
flooding my mind, my soul, my loins with the need
to express myself in manners proper and necessary.

damn you for awakening me.
I had surrendered to my prison and laid down to die
and you decided that you wanted to see if the legends
were true and my wings were still able to blot out the sun
as I wrapped you in them and carried you to the top
of Mount Aetna,
to be ravished as in the legends I thought were myths,
having lost my faith in the gods of love and their child,
now a woman of comely form and wicked wiles who dares
to summon me from my tomb to fulfill our union.

damn you for awakening me.
your cries of passion and fear and tenderness burn away
my doubts and I am now more phoenix than golem.
I am now more the hungry heat, incarnate, than thought,
roaring my spells of summoning to draw you closer.
we melt and merge
and the prophesies never told us what happens next beyond
a general sense of a happy ever after ending, our spark struck
to burn eternal in the hearts of all brave enough to look up
and see your beauty in the bowl of the sun, reborn as I am.

I'm not going anywhere

I'm not going anywhere.
Well, not on a vector remotely away from you
in the long run.
I plan to stick around,
cheer you on in all life's little competitions,
pick up the pieces
when you get blindsided .
It isn't that you need me, but that I want you
to have the advantage.

So I'll sit in this comfy chair,
you know the one, and see what happens next.
And after that.
See if you see your way clear,
not because you are unmotivated now, but truthfully,
there's a lot
we have to deal with.
Yet I'm not running, but standing my ground, standing around,
waiting for your blessing, to begin.

I can only say what I know

I can only say what I know.
There is a point where desire and love are shallow words
but we are loath to confess our needs.
Need, the unwillingness to go without.
Oxygen, water, food and your love.

Not love itself, for so many sins
are committed in the blank slate that hangs fate on a word
so that trouvere may sing memories.
But you. Your love. The heated sweet cinnamon
of your eyes and thighs and no disguise.

You are naked to me, beyond metaphor.
All attempts to cast you as cat or stone or mythic beast
is a waste of my soul, you are your own legend.
And as I confess the crackling flames of lust
and soft adoration, you are as a fulcrum.

in this bed

in this bed your maidenhead is certain to be found.
a new release, a perfect peace, a love without relent.
for in my life and in my soul, I am forever bound
to you alone, and we atone our follies, my lament
is reconciled, my lover and child, born of ancient dream.
touching in fashions transcending our passions, joy
and revelation, resolution and revolution perfecting theme
of love transcending the shallows, the parapets of Troy,
thrown down in the name of the arrogance of man
to think that what is divine can be touched and held.
you are here because you chose to be, the purpose and plan
of love fulfilled, a consecration, illumination. what was felled
is risen and given as sacrifice to the gods of love, who nod
a beatific grace to acknowledge the presence of a wise and merciful God.

your love is a revelation

your love is a revelation. a purifying spirit
that consumes me in a pillar of fire and light.
I learn from the universe the nature of love.
I learn from the universe the nature of dreams.
a perfect epiphany. a perfected epiphany.
your beauty and faith and earnest touch
is a gift I could never be worthy of, your love
is spiritual and physical and mine, by grace.

the bitter herbs

the bitter herbs
taste better with Kool-Aid
so I can wash them down
and get
another paper cup
another paper cup
and I tell myself that I can't taste
the bitter herbs

but

they were there
they left a strange sensation
in my belly
and smelled of
cinnamon
kisses
and the colour of your lips
at an indecent distance

so

I can say I took
my wormwood, but I never really
tasted it
like I did your sweat
long nights trying so hard to say
that for which there are no words
just the magic of your touch
incendiary

and

I need to be immolated
desecrated by your passions
given and received
in the music box of memory
wet with our hungers
to feel anything
to taste anything
to know anything

for sure
for ever

teach me of your mythologies

teach me of your
mythologies.
the legends
that you see
dance
when you close your eyes
and realize
that reality
is just another excuse
for the cynicism of others.
for Plato said
this is all shadows.
but I
have great peripheral vision
and have been known
to move my neck
enough
to see things most
can't or won't.
I need
a frame of reference
whether it is
Aphrodite or Venus
or another pantheon,
altogether,
so that I do not
defile your temples
(in a bad way)
or utter
insecure profanities.
this is important to me,
as you are,
and I would know my place
in heaven
and feel secure
I will always
wake up in your arms,
and you in mine.

some insist that vows are mad

some insist that vows are mad
take what you can and run, they say.
I don't want to live that way.
those who do, they make me sad.
romance is not found in spark
we play at being lovers for.
the shadows dance by, by the score,
they flicker out in solemn dark.
alone I sit, a vow to clutch.
alone, and yet with more than most.
a dignity, not memory's ghost,
I gamble all for your honest touch.
dreams are but for waking from.
I want your all. for it I've come.

and when all things that ever mattered

and when all the things that ever mattered
are in the meadow, by treasons scattered,
I'll smile a thought and catch a memory
on sweetness not a mocking travesty.
a gentle touch, an earnest kiss we share,
the way you brush the moments from your hair.
I lay awake and watch you dance for me,
a perfect moment trapped in memory.
these times are ours, from idle eyes we shield
the naked hearts and fantasies revealed.
upon this bed we pledge our sacrifice.
for all we gain, this bartered Pascal's price.
and when we part it will be tapestry
we wove together, our meld history.

this is not a place of skulls

this is not a place of skulls,
but of flesh
and the infinite possibilities of life
seized at the perihelion,
fire and power
flowering like your heart in a kiss
surrendered to.
remembered in time,
precognizant memory
and a possession
of what was already held,
a symbol of the sweet baptism
and the transcendence
of brave and constant hearts,
words unleashed
to preach to us
the gospel of innocence.
burn me with your beauty,
make the duty of my vows
a joy for as long as I walk,
as long as my soul inhabits this sphere,
making way for the next
and a place for you there,
if that is your will,
as it is mine.

I will trust you under Heaven

I will trust you under Heaven.
I will trust you with my heart.
I will trust you to be faithful
and to never tear apart
all the fragile, earnest windings
that we're weaving with our prayers,
all the bright and lambent findings
that can purge the past nightmares.
All I ask is that you trust me
just a little, till I'm proved
as one who offers honesty
with his passion and has soothed
all the earnest, learn'd doubts you have picked up on the path
to this moment, where I pledge, I will give no cause to wrath.

faith and hope

faith and hope.
prayers and sacraments.
the frame of a new religion.
a better religion.
love.
accepting, forgiving.
wanting to be part.
willing to surrender.

God is in the details.
I don't know enough
and even if I did, would I trust
my own judgment?
Not likely.

a word. a promise or two.
a broken promise
is not a lie
unless it is made in vain.
but I believe you,
because you just seem right.

right for me.
not a perfect fit, in the classic sense,
but someone I have been
in training for, all my life.
someone whose incongruities
excite me.

I would be the same for you.
my deepest, coldest fear
is that you will tire of me,
for that would break my heart.
my patchwork work.
all the scars already.

I believe in you
as I believe in God,
more than I believe in myself.
when you say "I love you"
it feels like I have done something
very, very good with my life.

I'll wait for you on the cusp of the night

I'll wait for you on the cusp of the night,
see you walk between shadows and the day.
I'll lay with you with passionate delight,
at the dawn, if you'll have me, I will stay.
Often lovers lie even with that word,
blaspheming for a solitary touch.
I am not here for purpose you've not heard
from my lips, testament of just how much
I want to linger into the light, days
becoming nights, becoming years and life.
I want to know you in all earthly ways,
embrace you in the manner of a wife.
And all of this is but one moment's thought,
but one that I know will not be forgot.

your breath when you sleep

your breath when you sleep
is so reassuring to me
evidence of a God who would
even if just for one moment
foretell heaven in my life
as you lay beside me
dreaming your arrogant dreams
your body warm and soft
to my trespass touch, bold
am I. bold and passionate
about you, my princess.
my goddess. my queen.

Does your lover know you talk with me

Does your lover know you talk with me
(the tears you've cried over them and more)
late at night, when they can't see
(as they tread on you, as if the floor
were higher up in their purview
and you were just now passing through.)
Do you know how much that breaks my heart
to know that they think love is rage
and you allow them, for their part,
for you conceive no way to gauge
the truth when pain is all you've known
as part of love, you've never been shown
the mercy that is passion's kiss
when raising up your hopes for real
and prayerfully, the arrows miss
for lovers guard you with their steel
and share with you all that is theirs
and elevate you and your cares
to heights of elegance and grace.
(with tenderness and faith's report)
They kiss the wounds and touch your face
and never make of you their sport.
For love is twisted by the bent
and simplified when heaven sent.

The light is red and turning to the grey

The light is red and turning to the grey
the sun is set and resting for the while
I turn to you and ask you for this last day
I turn to you and ask you for your smile.
The moments bend and befriend us for now.
The moments melt like snow on eager grass.
The night has come and left with us a vow
to let us rest as lovers in stained glass.
I hold you near and need no other ease.
I hold you near and feel the fears unwind.
I pray that God will leave us, each to please
and will, in sins forgiveness, be most kind.
I do not know for certain many things.
I only know the peace your presence brings.

Sweep

the curve, the nerve.
don't hit the nerve.
the blood is all we're after
the laughter of pain
the stain on sheets
the endorphin feedback loop
that little death hidden
in a scar
that perfects the sweetness
with a facet to be traced
by tear and raging rut.
I would kiss the flesh
and draw away the venom.
not to make it go away
but to share it.
and take it into me
to have something
undeniably
in common
with the dark woman
with the nightshade eyes
and a scar
or two
or ten thousand
to mark truth worth touching

lyric: romanticism

as the sun
traces fire across the sky
I smile into your heart
and hope to never die

for memory is no better
than a fantasy
truth just hopes you'll set her
to her destiny

we are not forgiven
any more than we forgive
we'll never know the answers
if we refuse to live

and I am waiting for you
with a dream forever new
and offer you no riddles
just a place where words are true

imagination

my imagination knows you too well.
the sound you make when I touch you, gently,
the feel of your body, curled into mine.
the tone of your voice when the words are fell:
but how they are spoken, reverently,
making me aware of divine design
in my encountering you, this frail shell
nothing but vessel for my light and heat.
paramour who conjures you as lover
and friend, companion and peer, fires of Hell
and the kiss of redemption, bittersweet.
I close my eyes and dream to discover
your presence where hope cast a patient spell.

Addiction

I want you to suffer from my withdrawal.
feeling lost inside.
the throbbing glide denied
until you demand your next fix
with wicked smile and earnest guile
to lure me again, willingly,
to flood your veins with my alchemy.
my base metal turned to gold as you hold
me deep, hungry for the rush, the flush
that leaves a deep and satisfying aftertaste
in both our mouths, evidence
that it was more for you than another pill.
another drag.
another sip of the nectar of forbidden fruit
that made your muscles ache and, awake,
made you walk in the land of dreams,
allowing me to taste you, to waste you.
not on carnival sideshow rides
but the full, merged and surged encouraged
purging purpose for which, even now,
I dream of in wicked prick'd metaphor
of an injection of my crude fluid
inside you to elevate your thighs high
to a dance of fire and desire sated.
only for the moment.
I want to be your drug, your addiction.
the friction of our flesh meshing messages
to our ancient brains, caught between moments
of civilized conduct that reassure us
that this is more than mere white blood
and the maddening taste of jasmine tea.

Satin Chessboard

I'll provide the fire.
I'll provide the light.
you provide the battlefield on which we'll spend the night.

you will bring your passion,
mine will be there, too.
I shall bring a tenderness
to share and comfort you.

I'll provide the questions.
you'll provide the thought.
I'll provide the formulae
to unbind the Gordian knot.

you will bring the red wine.
I will bring the white.
but in the darkness which is which
will be hidden from our sight.

I will play the suitor.
you will play what role
you choose in moments to defend
your flesh, your heart, your soul.

I will lay as sacrifice,
leaving nothing but to your will
to play this satin chessboard
with your purpose and your skill.

I'll provide the fire.
I'll provide the light.
you provide the battlefield on which we'll spend the night.

Exhortation

take control. take my soul.
there is no more illusion.
naught to lose, if you choose,
the heat of perfect fusion.

edges melt, a fever felt,
impurities vaporizing.
strike the spark. split the dark.
we fall to birth a rising.

In praise of precognition

I have and will love with fierce devotion,
emotion layered upon itself, born
in respect, in a genuflection
upon a desire, a fire, torn
from the heart of the sun itself, a heat
so intense it makes mock of memory.
It burns away the pain, the incomplete,
the scars that others left in sorry
semblance of their lives, wounds to cauterize
with a persistent, insistent brisance.
A healing kiss long time coming. Arise
as does the Sunday sun, to live and dance
with a passion that blinds Prometheus
and renders lesser flesh extraneous.

I dreamt about you

I dreamt about you
before you were born.
so maybe prayers get answered
anyway.

you're here, at last,
and you say you're gonna stay.
if so, that's the best news
I've ever heard.

you're inconvenient
in so many ways.
that's why you suit me fine,
and perfectly.

you're unexpected
like the summer rain,
and just as necessary.
at least for me.

lyric: everything and more

I feel a rush
whenever I see your name
your voice cuts deep
and reaches me in my sleep
your sultry smile
makes me think of your kiss and touch
not asking for much
just everything
and more

I feel your eyes
even when I am miles away
your presence bends
around walls and distance that
we will break down
in time and trust and heat and all
not asking for much
just everything
and more

I want your word
and what it means to you
you are a drug
and my veins burn when you're away
I need you now
and there's no methadone
not asking for much
just everything
and more

Ceremonies of our nature

We are all creatures of habit
reassured by repetition, repetition.
Fitting our lives into boxes
that we might better guard hearts from recognition
by those who seek only prey.
By those who cut and tear with evil ambition.

Stormweaver

gonna make a believer
even out of the deceiver.
gonna break and take and wake
the foundations of the earth, to make
the skies light up, explode and arc
with the fire you inspire, ripping up the dark.
translating the vision for the blind and unkind
who've never really seen it and will find
it alien to their understanding, heat and light
from the same source, the full course, night
flowing into day into life and splitting infinity.
stormweaving by the power of will, making trinity
the pop of an indifferent champagne cork. power
is the prerogative of the fearless, the flower
of creation is found beyond where we die.
I cannot be bound but by the sound as I try
to use words to explain why I am here, closing
the gap, cutting the crap, the slap of posing
against cold stone idols that failed the test.
a copper conductor becomes the terminus, blest
by the possibilities and defiance of dogmas
of what is to become of the fallen, the laws
of nature not knowing what we can do, proud,
with a handful of rain and the friction of clouds.

Fit in Me

fit in me
break the metaphor of penetration and find inside me
a place to face yourself
the you I see so perfectly
independent of the scar tissue
or perhaps because of it.
the light scintillates as it reflects
off of what others have called
flaws
and I call
you

the you I want inside me
sheltered
and secure
pure to the diatomaceous earth
that so many writhe in
trying to get clean when
they already are

I have been to the stars
more times than you have kissed lips
you really didn't love
just because it felt awkward
to say "No" after dinner.
I have stood in airless space
and contemplated the cold
as it creeps into me
with no real purpose
just nature

I want you inside me
filling me
willing me to love again
an unconditional love
and kissing your scars
and the curve of your thighs
and anything else
that needs kissing
to prove my ardor and respect

you are beautiful.
and diamonds are but coal crushed
until it gives up the illusion of darkness
and powder and blossoms
into a crystal
I would gladly buy for you
sight unseen, words unheard
no matter it sounds absurd
it is balance to the universe

tuck yourself in
make yourself comfortable
strap yourself in
and grab on
I can ride the shock waves of magnetars
if you provide the meaning
to the exploration
of corners of myself
and you
and the extrapolated God

the snows have melted
and run away to rivers and mud puddles,
nevermore the pristine white
that once blanketed creation
so it is left to us to reclaim innocence
the innocence of wisdom
but you can call me Daddy if you want

I will not change my heart
but place it on course
irrevocable and sure
and trusting in you
because there is something
something
something there
beyond sweet lips and quick wit

fit in me
for I am incomplete
and it is not a crowbar job
for you to slide into the grooves
that are still waiting for the right fit
the right person
the right woman
the one who can forgive me
and herself
for things best left at the altars
when I stand still for you

and you climb inside

intimacy

what care have I of moments outside
of these,
where I please you and you speak
the inarticulate language of love.
dreams in a kiss
windows in the darkness
the writhing of mingled beings
being what they choose
not losing in the loosing
of the bindings of lace
that I might raise you to me
as I seek only to give to you
all my fire and desire
for you are mine and fine
as the wine I drank from you
between the warm thighs I delight in,
kissing and missing no curve and fold
that informs you of my passion.
I will be your lover
when light without heat fades.
and leave my mark inside you
to guide you closer to the man
who would bind himself to you
for the truth he has found.
and you are beautiful.

So once again

so once again there's an electric lady,
to challenge me my purpose and my dreams.
shall I dissolve again into the ether?
shall I resolve the conflict, as it seems?

I once gave up my poor and mortal birthright
that I might touch the sky and see true things.
I am stronger yet and wiser, well, and so
my choice, my voice, is now not waxen wings.

so once again there's an electric lady.
the light so bright it burns deep, with sweet heat,
an apocalypse that so gamely trips
into my world, my arms, the suite now complete.

bring me what you care and dare and bear to share,
I am unafraid. Stronger now, I would take
you into my sphere and pour myself out,
like waterglass, and loving vows ne'er forsake.

for the final time, my electric lady,
I stand before you in this human shell.
begging redemption, no pretension,
I would not, your tender love, to say farewell.

your resolute

you can leave me to die
but I will not, can not,
for that is blasphemy
to my purpose, my vow.
planets may yet shatter,
constellations scatter
it will be no matter.
I am your resolute.

the sun will burn my flesh
and the cold will numb me.
fading thought will dumb me
down to the snapped masses.
I am given to stand
and to offer my hand
to my promises' command.
I am your resolute.

I am throwback to grace
of a different time
a different place where
courtly love was the code.
defiant to the gates
where Orpheus awaits,
the champion of fates.
I am your resolute.

No apologies

you said
no apologies
and I embrace that
we don't owe the world
anything
but the echo of our heat
drying on sheets
and in the wind

words
consecrating passion
the memory of life
the purpose of life
the beauty of you
pressed like a flower
in the book
I am still writing
because you came along
when I thought I was done
and undid the last chapter
into a whole new arc
full of mystery and fantasy
and love and shadows
and I am grateful
for every excruciating second
as the clock counts down
to a purpose
for which I will not apologize

except to you,
for my having taken so long
to get here

Another hollow midnight

another hollow midnight
these are the times
when I wish I'd liked the taste
of that first cigarette
something to do with my hands
my mouth
my money
besides sitting here
sitting here
like a deflated toy balloon
to avoid pacing
or curling up in the corner
and finding solace
in shadows

another hollow midnight
it's not that she's
not here
obviously
because the sheets are straight
and there is no telltale
outline
of where she fell
with me on top
finding my way

another hollow midnight
it's that she chooses
not to be here
and I can't argue
with her logic, because she's right
we make no sense
at all
but that's the way
the heart chooses
to speak its mind

another hollow midnight
reflecting on the cigarettes
I never smoked
the memories I never had
and the dry air
that swirls up around me
when it should be
wet and clinging
like lips and hips and hands
when lovers
want something
something more
something true

another hollow midnight
I think I'll write a poem
and tell the world
how it hurts like glass shards
under my tongue
in my heart
and there are no ashtrays
anyway
if I wanted to smoke
just those mocking sheets
where I laid the rose petals
as if to summon her
when I knew the odds
all along

I will write for a while
then lay down
let the petals wither
let my words ferment
congeal and spoil
before I flush them
like used condoms
from a prophylactic heart
used to the feel
of latex instead of flesh
but hating it all the while
romantics
don't like the secret handshake
of those who don't understand
another hollow midnight

cleansing the wound

alone against the rocks I lay.
broken. roadkill, but for final breath.
no more dreams, no dragons to slay.
I am just waiting for the death
that promises its loyal blade
in prophecies and tributes sung,
a morbid, maddening song is played,
and we slide in beneath the dung.
for comes a time when passions fade
and grey possess all we held.
when sacraments are mocked, betrayed
by dark illusions, echoes welled
in tears of pain to taunt the path
and sell to us a coward's wrath.

Adversity

faith without challenge is not faith
love without tension is a wraith
of a ghost of a passion, untested.

I am pale and sick and lay alone,
but you have sworn greater stand
and I will lay alone in your name.

be well and strong, hurry back,
but do not short shrift that which requires
your attention and your focus.

I will wait, I promised. I do not wait
to keep the promise, but I promised
so you would know that I would wait.

patiently? as best as I can, like a man
who has tasted honey and then has none.
but content the feast will return.

To a lover

This is not for the cold catalepsies
but the pure warmth you can invoke
with a soft smile or the simplest ease
with words of truth and love. In you awoke
my slumbering passion, admiration
for this woman who steps into my life
with hesitant grace, elegance hard won
in her own sphere, now as near as a wife
though more than one reasoned season shall pass
before you may choose to lose your ronin
reputation to the gentle impasse
within sharing, caring, daring to win
whatever it is within my power
to grant to you. I am your dreams' bower.

Matthew 6:16

My love is a constant thing.
Unbroke by words that may fall
from your weary lips and heart.
I celebrate you then and
ask for nothing less than life
with you beside me and strong.

There will come some storms and pain.
There will come some night and rain.
There will come the wax and wane.
But you never need doubt me.
I am given not to fade
in the face of the harsh lights.

You are still so beautiful.
I can recall soft words spoke
that burned and churned my heart's quick.
So bring to me your edge, hard
and hack me a little bit.
In love, resilient, strong
I will remain your lighthouse.

That you ever may find me
watching over you, even
when you don't think you need it,
as that is my nature, love,
that is the nature of love.
And I am of its nature.
For you, and with you, alone.

Chastity

surrender me your chastity
I'll give you all I've left
to fill your aching soul with me
and taste your tender cleft.

I'll answer to your fantasies
I've sins yet to atone
with tender touch and savageries
to make of you, mine own.

I want to be your satyr king,
your lover, daddy, prince.
I want to find you swallowing
every hot and throbbing inch.

And when we lay in aftermath,
in completed, heated rests,
we've miles to go along this path,
I'll kiss your perfect breasts.

When at length we resurrect
and wake to find our thirst
reawakened by our wild aspect,
we'll sate again this curse.

I will never ask your grace
to let me taste one trace
of another's heat and sweet disgrace,
for I know my need and place.

Lighthouse

I want to be your lighthouse
I want to stand alone
in the darkest storms that threaten
to break your every bone
and throw you up upon the reefs
your sails all ripped to shred
I want to be your lighthouse
and defy the raging dread
of the past and all its thunder
the liars and the lost
who just wanted to be with you
no matter what the cost
to your vanity and sanity
your sanctity and joy
crushing you beneath their fury
like a child's ocean liner toy.
I want to be your lighthouse.
I want to stand for you
I want to be hold aloft the light
that you can follow, to get through.
I want to be your lighthouse.
I want to be relief
from the terrors that consume
your sleep in black and burning grief.

heptahedron

there is an ebb and flow to passions that would grow.
tenderness and the dire and carnal need to feed.
sharing breath and the petty death until we live.
I may claim you but never tame you, I am yours.
patience earned and learned, until fleshes run rampant.
burn me, turn me into what you most need, I bleed.
precious mettle, bright as ten thousand emeralds.

lost at a cost

moments run like sand between fingers
too gnarled with age
too unpracticed in the sphere of Venus
tests of will and wonder
time will tell anyone who listens
what became of them
and whether the pronoun
needs capitalized
or even explained
Orpheus draws deep breath
taught to him in another aeon
to stir coeur rage like memories
not yet made
but possible
if you can rise above
the ruins of a Babylon
where the costs of certainty
included ignorance
and the music is perfect

witness

your light persists, even though bent a bit
by the refracting forces of history and mystery.
passions like a thousand fires on the face of the sun,
you run light and bright into the night, immortal.
I am but an observer, your witness to the world
that might otherwise rest dull and dumb, uninspired
by ignorance of the fires that dance across your skin.
you are, by any measure, remarkable, perfect padparadscha
regardless of the wit and wisdom of those who see
and do not comprehend your worth and wonder.
you are memory and prophecy, beauty and truth,
the one I have waited for, and will wait for,
even until the end of all things. all things.
for you asked me to wait, to linger, to learn patience
that I might be there when you whisper my name.

Xerophyte

In times I have writ
more than my fair share
to tumbleweed muses.
Blown by the winds
of their own fears and egos
cluttering the highways
with lifeless branches.
Bartering nothing to purpose
that sustains the pains and light
but dry and tasteless illusions
ultimately cluttering the landscape.
I have misperceived their motion
in the wind for life and truth.
Burn them down and see what remains.

Roadkill blues

if you consider the overlapping timeframes
I have been friend zoned more than I have been alive on this planet
which is I guess is a little depressing
but at the same time it is nice that people think I am a nice person
(not that nice)
I do miss being connected
in more than just the physical sense
although…
I am not complaining
but I do tend to become friends
and I have lots of friends
some of whom know I have or had
at one time or another
crushes on them
some of them do not have a clue

my books are full of thousands of poems to women
who decided we'd be better off as friends
and that is how the story often ends

unpleasant

but it's how it goes
but you have to give people the right to choose their own path
the person who says "no"
has control
that is how it should be
that is how it always should be
and we should accept that
so wherever you are
whatever you are doing
be thankful for those who did not always give you
everything you wanted from the relationship
they are exercising their freedoms
and trusting you to respect theirs

TRIUMPH

Carry back the fallen, they are now no more than obstacles and eyesores on the battlefields,
worthy hearts that met their fates as fodder to a purpose yet obscure and oblique, seeking no
validation for their immolation in the fireflower field that sealed their epitaphs in eclectic blue and red,
steady hands on the rudder of the boat that sails the River Styx and picks its way through carrion
feeding the lampreys of lethargy and the lachrymal leeches that bloat on their own poisons flowed
like rows of roses mowed down in a mad gardener's harvest of slash and burn horticulture.

Carry back the fallen, for they deserve proper burial away from the emotions of this carnage,
this new age of children playing make-believe around the grieving truths that emasculate dreams
in the sad, seamless shroud of a religion of the damned. We are the vanguard and the residual force,
the dessert course for the ghouls that pick their way through the bazaar banquet tables of the dead.
Heroes have fled to lick their wounds and toast their victories, leaving us to save what we can
of the sanity we possessed before Odin chose to wrest from us the wisdom traded for a single eye.

Carry back the fallen, for in this season we possess not the reason to understand their sacrifice,
pain raining down like the tears of hungry children we'd rather buy a book of lies than feed for our need
is so selfish, our pain so intimate, our terror so consummate, our dreams so delicate they will shatter
with the first touch of a gloved hand, standing without legs in a room without a floor in a world without God,
getting even with the odds we set when we wet our whetstones and honed our sharp tongues to lance
like a poignard into the heart of the matter that will shatter and scatter us like the debris of freedom.

Carry back the fallen, for they need not see what next I do. For the victory is of more import than my life.
Where blades have bent, I have sent them back to the fire to be reforged as steel, not pig-iron, tempered
by the winds I call in necromancies dark and deadly, I said we would triumph, and so we shall. Hide
your face from the light I call, for I will not take responsibility for your soul, crusaders come and go and
slowly we have earned every inch of our position in this game of rogues and wizards, but only one song
will be sung when the histories are recited tonight around a bright bonfire of sacred woods and thistles.

Carry back the fallen. For then will I be alone, without the staring eyes of the dreamers locked forever
in a hidden instant. Incant me the words I swore to take to war if love and fear would ever go sour, the power
is not a madman's riddle, but the middle of the sphere where nearly all of us hide our chitinous mantras,
enchanted with our own venoms and vindications, paying reparations for a trail of abominations we would
tell lies to hide from the child inside us, growing on our virtues and our sins to be stillborn as we have torn
our own amniotic sacs to force our way into a world where few get out alive, striding in baby steps.

Carry back the fallen. And I will be among them. And there will be no songs tonight, no dances to mark
this victory. For in triumph, we are all victims of our own basest natures, fated to mate with the incubi
and succubi of our own vanity. The only war worth fighting is in our own hearts and souls. Horatius died
a suicide, in some philosophies. Think what you please, dream what you will, say what you must, but dust
still dries a poet's tongue to the point that the words are only words and the word I heard a lifetime ago
must now ultimately sleep or perish, beneath a metaphor'd field I once heard of...barren with snow.

About the Author

William F. DeVault has, in his creative run (so far) amassed tens of thousands of poems (and those are just the ones that passed first reading). He has published over 20 books, received his unfair share of sobriquets, and performed his poetry all over the continental United States and throughout cyberspace. He has read in churches, bars, parks, schools, libraries, and brothels.

Married twice, divorced twice, but still the romantic optimist, he has fathered three children in whom he is well pleased, and mentored dozens of poets. He founded and lead the **Romantic and Erotic Poetry Group** for America Online, and that service's **Passionate Craft** poetry workshop.

He was named the **Romantic Poet of the Internet** by Yahoo in 1996 and the **US National Beat Poet Laureate** by the National Beat Poetry Foundation for 2017-2018. Some consider him the **Poet Laureate of the Internet** for his presence and pioneering use of the internet during and even before the mid-1990's. He is a founding member in the **Rolling Stock Poets**.

www.ingramcontent.com/pod-product-compliance
Lightning Source LLC
Chambersburg PA
CBHW081134300726
48982CB00005B/969

* 9 7 8 1 7 3 4 9 4 6 9 2 5 *